GLEAMS OF TRUTH
Prescriptions for a Healthy Social Life

THE RISALE-I NUR COLLECTION

GLEAMS OF TRUTH
Prescriptions for a Healthy Social Life

BEDİÜZZAMAN SAİD NURSİ

Translated by Hüseyin Akarsu

New Jersey

Published by Tughra Books
345 Clifton Ave., Clifton,
NJ, 07011, USA

www.tughrabooks.com

Library of Congress Cataloging-in-Publication Data Available

ISBN 978-1-59784-214-3 (hardcover)

Printed by
Çağlayan A.Ş., Izmir - Turkey

Table of Contents

PART FOUR

Preface

Bediüzzaman Said Nursi &
Prescriptions for a Healthy Social Life

HE LEGACY OF BEDIUZZAMAN SAID NURSI'S (1877–1960) achievements, personality and character, and his continuing influence make him an important figure in the twentieth-century Muslim world. In a most effective and profound way Bediüzzaman represents Islam's intellectual, moral, and spiritual strengths. He spent most of his life overflowing with love and ardor for Islam, employing a wise activism that is based on sound reasoning, and which was developed in the shade of the Qur'an and the Prophetic example.

Much has been said and written about the lofty ideals which he pursued and his deep familiarity with the world and his times, as well as his simplicity and austerity, human tenderness, loyalty to friends, chastity, modesty, and contentedness.

Though strikingly simple in outward appearance, many of his ideas and activities are wholly original. He embraced humanity and was deeply opposed to unbelief, injustice, and deviation; Bediüzzaman strove against all kinds of tyranny, even at the cost of his life. His profound belief and feeling, when combined with his wise and rational ideas, and his problem-solving methods, produced an example of love, ardor, and feeling. He was extraordinarily balanced in his thoughts, acts, and methods of dealing with various matters; Said Nursi was a far-sighted man who assessed and judged the surrounding conditions and tried to solve the problems confronting him.

Many of his contemporaries acknowledged, either tacitly or explicitly, that Bediüzzaman was the most important thinker and writer of the twentieth-century Turkey, or even of the Muslim world. Despite this and his indisputable place in a new Islamic revival in the intellectual, social, and political conditions of his time, he remained a humble servant of God. His life exemplified his understanding of humility: "Desire for fame is the same as show and ostentation, and it is a 'poisonous honey' that extinguishes the vitality of the heart."

Born in a small mountain village in eastern Turkey, Bediüzzaman voiced the sighs and laments of the entire Muslim world, as well as its belief, hopes and aspirations. He said:

> I can bear my own sorrows, but the sorrows that arise from the calamities visited upon Islam and Muslims have crushed me. I feel each blow delivered to the Muslim world as if it were delivered first to my own heart. That is why I have been so shaken.

He also said:

> During my life of over eighty years, I have tasted no worldly pleasure…. There has been no persecution I have not tasted, no oppression I have not suffered. I neither care for Paradise nor fear Hell. If I see my nation's faith secured, I will not even care about burning in Hell, for while my body is burning, my heart will be as if in a rose garden.

Bediüzzaman lived at a time of global crisis. Materialism was at its peak, Communism had a wide following, and Muslims were being urged to reject Islam. Shocked by the West's scientific and military victories, and influenced by modern thought, Muslims were discarding their historical roots and sometimes their faith. Many Muslim intellectuals deviated from the Straight Path. Bediüzzaman, however, directed people to the source of belief and inculcated in them a strong hope for an overall revival. His writings displayed the truth of Islam and opposed the growing deviation.

At a time when science and philosophy were being used to produce young atheists and Nihilism was popular, when such things were done in the name of civilization, modernization, and contemporary thinking,

Bediüzzaman strove for the overall revival of a people, breathing into their minds and spirits both modern and traditional education as well as spiritual training.

Bediüzzaman diagnosed the long-standing "diseases" that afflicted the Muslim communities and offered the most effective cures. Basing his activity on the Qur'an, the Sunna, the Islamic tradition, and natural phenomena (considered to be signs of Divine Existence and Unity), he concentrated, in order of importance, on supporting the pillars of Islam; the necessity of belief, worship, morality, and good conduct, as well as discovering the socio-economic issues facing contemporary Muslims.

The Essence of Bediüzzaman's Thinking and Activities

During Bediüzzaman's time and our own, ignorance of God and the Prophet, upon him be peace and blessings, heedlessness of religious commandments, indifference to the Islamic dynamics of prosperity in both worlds, and ignorance of modern scientific knowledge have been among the primary factors of the backwardness of the Muslim world. Bediüzzaman maintained that if Muslims did not acquire modern scientific and religious knowledge or the ability to think systematically, and if they could not protect themselves against misleading trends of thought by acquiring true knowledge, they would never escape the backwardness into which they had fallen.

Ignorance was a source of Muslim poverty. Ignorance of the truth of Islam, when added to the ignorance of scientific and technological knowledge, resulted in vast plains remaining uncultivated and the natural wealth of Muslim lands flowing into the treasuries of others. Ignorance was a major reason for the internal conflicts of the Muslim world, as well as other problems. Although the Qur'an demands unity, Muslims were quarreling with each other even as their lands were being invaded by foreign forces and their people were being humiliated.

At the same time, those Muslim intellectuals to whom the masses looked for leadership and salvation were attracted by the violent storm of denial that blew in from the West. Emerging in previous centuries from a humanity-centered world-view that was rooted in scientism, rationalism, and positivism, as well as from the contradictions between modern scientific findings and a Church opposed to science, this storm gradually robbed Europe of most of its belief in Christianity. Consequently, the Revelation was forced to yield to human reason.

This process, unparalleled in history, shook the "edifice" of Islam, which was already perceived as being old and decayed in many hearts and minds (both individual and communal), to its roots. Bediüzzaman believed that this "edifice" could be preserved from further destructive influences by presenting the essentials of Islam, with all its branches, to the minds and reason of modern men and women. According to him, the Muslim world, so clearly beached on the oceans of the modern world, would be able to sail freely again only if it underwent a successful, comprehensive renewal in all fields of Islam.

Bediüzzaman dedicated himself to expounding the pillars of Islam. Anti-Islamic trends and attitudes among intellectuals and the young, as a result of a deliberately positivist – even materialist – system of education, were on the rise. These factors forced Bediüzzaman to concentrate on the essentials of belief and worship and the main purposes that were pursued in the Qur'an, which he described as explaining and proving Divine Existence and Unity, Prophethood, Resurrection, and the necessity of worship and justice. He explains:

> The highest aim of creation and its most sublime result is belief in God. The most exalted rank of humanity is knowledge of God. The most radiant happiness and sweetest bounty for jinn and humanity is love of God contained within the knowledge of God; the purest joy for the human spirit and the purest delight for the human heart is the spiritual ecstasy contained within the love of God. Indeed, all true happiness, pure joy, sweet bounties, and unclouded pleasure are contained within the knowledge and love of God.
>
> Belief is not restricted to a brief affirmation based on imitation; rather, it has degrees and stages of expansion or development. It is like a seed growing into the state of a fully grown, fruit-bearing tree, or like the sun's image in a mirror or in a drop of water to its images on the sea's surface and to the sun itself. Belief contains so many truths pertaining to all the Names of God and the realities contained in the universe that the most perfect human science, knowledge, and virtue is belief and knowledge of God that originates in a belief based on argument and investigation. While belief based on imitation can be refuted through doubt and ques-

tions raised by modern thought, belief based on argument and investigation has as many degrees and grades of manifestation as the number of Divine Names. Those who attain certainty of belief coming from direct observation of the truths on which belief is based study the universe as a kind of Qur'an.

The Qur'an, the universe, and humanity are three different manifestations of one truth. The Qur'an, having issued from the Divine Attribute of Speech, may be regarded as the universe written or composed. The universe, having originated in the Divine Attributes of Power and Will, may be considered as the Qur'an created. Since the universe is the counterpart of the Qur'an and, in one respect, the collection of Divine laws of creation, sciences that study the universe cannot be incompatible with Islam. Therefore, in the present time (when science prevails) and in the future (the age of knowledge), true belief should be based on argument and investigation, on continual reflection on God's "signs" in the universe, and on natural, social, historical, and psychological phenomena. Belief is not something based on blind imitation; rather, it should appeal to both the intellect/reason and the heart, for it combines the acceptance and affirmation of reason and the experience and submission of the heart.

There is another degree of belief, namely, certainty coming from direct experience of its truths. This depends on regular worship and reflection. One who has acquired such belief can challenge the entire world. So, our first and foremost duty is to acquire such belief and, in complete sincerity and purely for the sake of God, communicate it to others. A *hadith* relates that it is better for you if one embraces belief through you than for you to possess the entire world.

As scientific studies and uncountable experiences clearly show, what is dominant in the order of the universe and in the basic purposes of the All-Majestic Maker for its existence are good, beauty, and perfection. For every branch of science that studies the universe indicates such a magnificent order and perfection with the general principles on which it is based that minds cannot conceive of something better than this universe. It is also an observable and experienced fact that evil, ugliness, falsehood, and badness are secondary and subordinate in creation. They are not the purposes of creation; rather, they exist indirectly and as measures of comparison. For example, ugliness serves for beauty to be manifested in various forms and degrees. Evil, and even Satan, have been allowed to attack humans so that they may function as a means for the development and perfection of human beings. In short, ugliness and evil have been created to serve as means for universal beauty and good.

Good, perfection, and beauty are essential to the existence of the universe. So, humankind, who has sullied the earth with its injustices and unbelief, will not be able to go to non-existence without first suffering the punishment for such atrocities and then without being the means for the realization of the basic purposes for the existence of the universe (by observing the Divine order).

In short, Bediüzzaman argues that belief consists of acquiring Islam in its entirety.

Bediüzzaman saw that modern unbelief originated from science and philosophy. Paradoxically, the neglect of science and technology by Muslims is what had caused them to fall behind the West in economic and military fields. But the same science and technology that enabled the West to achieve global military and economic superiority had caused Western people to lose their faith and traditional moral and spiritual values, thus falling into pessimism, unhappiness, and spiritual crisis. This was natural, because although the Divine laws of nature (the subject-matter of science) are the counterpart of the Divine Scripture or Religion, they had been separated from one another in the West. Consequently, secular morality and economic self-interest had replaced religious and other traditional values. Bediüzzaman viewed nature as a collection of Divine signs, which meant that science and religion could not be in conflict; rather, they are two (apparently) different expressions of the same truth. Minds should be enlightened by science, while hearts need to be illumined by religion.

Bediüzzaman's prescriptions for a healthy social life

Bediüzzaman lived in a time of transition – the dying years of the Ottoman State and the formative years of the Turkish Republic. He completed the normal *medrese* (traditional religious school) education by the age of fourteen. However, even in his early years he was dissatisfied with the existing education system. Contrary to the centuries-old practice of religious scholars, he also studied natural and social sciences. He soon developed comprehensive proposals for reform, at the heart of which was his call for joining traditional religious sciences with modern secular sciences and establishing universities in major Turkish cities in which his proposals could be implemented. Although he twice received funds for his university and saw its foundations laid in 1913, it was never completed due to the consequences of the First World War and the vicissitudes of the time.

During the earlier period of his life which coincided with the last years of the Ottoman State, Bediüzzaman Said Nursi was involved in the socio-political life of the country. He traveled much, held meetings with Kurdish leaders and religious scholars in the south-east of Turkey, visited the Balkans and the Caucasus, and saw first-hand the ignorance, poverty, and internal conflict prevalent in Turkey and the greater Muslim world. He was in Istanbul when Sultan Abdülhamid II was dethroned and Constitutionalism was declared. He severely criticized despotism in all fields of life and supported a constitutionalism based on the Islamic principle of consultation. He wrote many books or booklets during these years, such as *Sunuhat* ("Occurrences to the Heart"), *Tulu'at* ("Flashes of Thoughts Rising in the Heart"), *Rumuz* ("Subtle Allusions"), *Isharat* ("Indications"), and *Munazarat* ("Discussions"). In these books or booklets, Bediüzzaman analyzed the condition of Muslims, the reasons why it was thus and discussed the ways this could be improved. He offered valuable prescriptions for a healthy social life. His two other books, *Hakikat Çekirdekleri* ("Seeds of Truths) and *Leme'at* ("Gleams of Truth – Flowers from Seeds of Truths"), in which he offered very valuable criteria for sound thinking, can also be included in this series of works.

In 1911, he delivered a sermon in the Umayyad Mosque in Damascus to approximately 10,000 people, including 100 high-ranking scholars. In this sermon which was later published under the title of *Khutba-i Shamiya* ("The Sermon of Damascus"), and in the other books mentioned, Bediüzzaman analyzes why the Muslim world had remained immured in the "Middle Ages": the growth of despair, the loss of truthfulness in social and political spheres, the love of belligerency and an ignorance of the bonds that is proper among believers, despotism in all fields of life, and egocentricity. He offered his cure: hope, truthfulness and trustworthiness, mutual love, consultation, solidarity, and freedom in accordance with Islam. He also emphasized the following points:

> History shows us that the development and civilization of Muslims
> is proportionate to their adherence to the truth of Islam, while the
> development and civilization of others is inversely proportionate

to their religion. Also, the truth informs us that the awakening of humankind cannot be without religion. Particularly, a person who has awakened to the truth, coming to know true humanity, and who is a candidate for the future and eternity, cannot be so without religion.

We Muslims, who are the students of the Qur'an, follow proof and accept the truths of belief with our reason, intellect, and heart. Unlike some members of other religions, we do not abandon proof or blindly imitate religious leaders. Therefore, in the future, when reason, sciences, and knowledge will dominate, it will be the Qur'an, the decrees and propositions of which are all confirmed by reason, that will certainly rule.

No period of history, from the Age of Happiness until the present time, tells us of a Muslim who has preferred another religion over Islam, based on sound reasoning, and entered that religion based on a sound proof. It is true that there have been some who have left Islam; but this has been through imitation and is of no importance. If we demonstrate the perfections of Islamic morality and the truth of Islam through our acts, the followers of other religions will continue to enter it in greater numbers; even some whole regions and countries of the earth will accept it.

Look, time does not move in a straight line so that its beginning and end grow distant from one another. Rather, like the movement of the earth, time moves by drawing a circle. It sometimes displays progress as an embodiment of spring and summer and sometimes displays decline as an embodiment of winter and a season of storms. So, just as every winter is followed by spring and every night by the morning, so too humankind will, God willing, also live a new morning and spring. From the Divine Mercy we can expect to see the true civilization marked by a general peace in the sun of the truth of Islam.

After the First World War, Bediüzzaman Said Nursi completely withdrew from socio-political life. He referred to himself when involved in socio-political life as the Old or Former Said, and now was wholly devoted to explaining the truths of Islamic faith and the meaning and importance of worship and good conduct. However, after 1950 he revised those works belonging to his earlier period, and published them again. This book in your hand is the translation of a compilation made from these works.

— Publisher

Part One

Part One

Seeds of Truth

In the Name of God, the All-Merciful, the All-Compassionate.

All praise be to God, and all blessing and peace be upon our master Muhammad, his Family, and Companions.

- The prescription for a diseased age, an ailing nation, and a disabled people is to follow the Qur'an.
- The prescription for this glorious, though unfortunate continent, once so illustrious, yet now a humbled and wretched state, once so invaluable, yet now an undefended people, is unity under the guidance of Islam.
- One who cannot turn the earth, planets, and stars as easily as turning the beads of a rosary cannot claim any part in creation, for everything is intertwined.
- The resurrection of all the dead on Judgment Day is as easy for God's Power as rousing a fly in the spring from its winter sleep. For the Divine Power is and inherent in the Divine Being; It cannot change, decay, diminish, or be impeded. Being absolute, It accepts no degrees and everything is equal in relation to It.
- The One Who has created the gnat's eye is He Who has created the sun.
- The One Who has ordered the flea's stomach is He Who has ordered the solar system.

- Seeing the universe's miraculous order and harmony, all "natural" causes (supposing they have independent agency) bow and say: "All-Glorified are You. We have no power. You are the All-Glorious, the All-Wise."

- As befits God's Oneness and Majesty, causes have no real or creative effect in creation or in the functioning of the universe. But in the outward (corporeal) dimension of existence, causes function to veil the operation of the Divine Power so that certain seemingly disagreeable or banal entities and events will not be attributed directly to It.

- The inner dimension of everything in which Divine Power operates directly is absolutely pure and transparent.

- This visible, corporeal world is a lace veil before the unseen worlds.

- Creating a dot in the right place requires an infinite power that can create the entire universe. Every letter of this great Book of the Universe, particularly every "living" letter, has a face turned toward and an eye gazing at every one of its sentences.

- At the end of one Ramadan, people were trying to catch sight of the new crescent moon that marks the beginning 'Iyd (the religious festive day). An old man claimed to see it. However, he did not know that what he saw was the curve of one of his own white eyelashes. How can an eyelash be equivalent to the crescent? How can the motion of minute atoms be accepted in place of the One Who forms entire species?

- Nature is a print or a model composed of unseen laws, but it is not the printer or composer. It is a design, not the designer, a recipient but not the agent; it is order, but not the one who puts things in order. It is a law, not a power. It is a collection of laws established by the Divine Will – the laws (that our minds can grasp but) that in themselves have no power or material reality.

- The feeling of attraction and being attracted felt in one's (innate) human conscience is due to the attractive power of the truth.

- A thing's innate drive or its God-given nature or disposition does not lie: For example, a seed's urge to grow says: "I will grow into such-and-such a plant and produce fruit," and then it does so. The urge for life in an egg tells it: "I will be a chick," and then it becomes a chick. The water's urge to freeze says: "I will take up more space," and then it does so. Hard and solid iron cannot contradict this; rather, when frozen, water can split iron. Such drives and urges are manifestations of the Divine commands of creation that issue from the Divine Will.

- The Eternal Power, Which ensures that ants have a leader and bees a queen, certainly would not deprive humanity of a Prophet's leadership. Splitting the moon was one of his miracles shown in the visible, corporeal world.[1] His Ascension (to God's "Presence")[2] was his greatest miracle shown to the angels and spirit beings in the World of Inner Dimensions, and one that proved and showed the saintliness of his Prophethood. Through that miracle, that most illustrious being extended and diffused his radiance, like a flash of lightning or a bright moon, in the World of Inner Dimensions.

- The two parts of the affirmation of belief – I bear witness that there is no deity but God, and I bear witness that Muhammad is His servant and Messenger – attest to each other's truth. The first is the a priori argument for the second, and the second is the a posteriori argument for the first.

- As life is a manifestation of unity in the sphere of multiplicity, it leads to unity, which enables one thing to own everything.

- The spirit is a law with consciousness and a real, sensible existence. Like enduring laws of creation, the spirit also issues from the World of Divine Commands and the Attribute of Will. Divine Power clothes the spirit in an astral body or double (the etheric counterpart of the physical body) within a body of sensory organs. This spirit, which exists in each human being, is a counterpart of the laws of

---

[1] Prophet Muhammad, upon him be peace and blessings, split the moon by a gesture of his index finger as a miracle he worked before a group of people who rejected his Prophethood in Makka. This is related in the most authentic Hadith sources, such as *Sahihu'l-Bukhari*, *Sahih Muslim*, and *Sunanu't-Tirmidhi*. The verses, *The Last Hour has drawn near, and the moon has split. Whenever they see a miracle, they turn from it in aversion and say: "This is sorcery like many others, one after the other."* (54:1–2) refer to this miracle. For a discussion about this miracle, see, Ali Ünal, *The Qur'an with Annotated Interpretation in Modern English*, The Light, New Jersey, 2008, pp. 1082–1083. (Tr.)

[2] The Ascension (*al-Mi'raj*): The miraculous journeying of Prophet Muhammad, upon him be peace and blessings, through the realms of existence beyond the limit of forms, during which he witnessed the supreme signs of God. For a discussion, see, Ali Ünal, *ibid.*, 1290–1295.

"nature," which have theoretical, invisible existence. Both are unchanging and permanent, and come from the World of Divine Commands. If Eternal Power had clothed laws with external existence, each would have been a spirit; if the human spirit were stripped of consciousness, it would become an immaterial law.

- Existent beings are visible by the agency of light, and their existence is known through life. Light and life are each discoverers and revealers.

- Christianity will either vanish or be purified and abandon its struggle against Islam. It has split several times and produced Protestantism which, in turn, has split (into diverse sects and groupings) and (some) have approached monotheism. Christianity will split further, after which it will disappear or, finding the truths of Islam, which include the essentials of Jesus' original religion, will follow Islam. This truth is indicated in a Prophetic Tradition: "Prophet Jesus will return to this world, join my community, and follow my Shari'a."[3]

- The majority of common people (the masses) are drawn by the sacredness of authority, rather than (the strength of) proofs.

- Ninety percent of the Shari'a consists of the essential and incontestable rules of Islam, and may be likened to diamond pillars. The remaining ten percent, which is open to interpretation and is to be determined by Islam's legal authorities, may be likened to gold pieces. Ninety diamond pillars cannot be put under the protection of ten gold pieces. Rather, the religious books and judicial arguments and judgments should help us to understand the Qur'an better. They should serve as binoculars to see and as mirrors to reflect its meanings, not to veil or replace it.

- Individuals qualified to practice ijtihad[4] can proclaim a new law for themselves, but not for others or the Muslim community.

- Before an idea related to the Religion can be extended to others, it must be accepted by the majority of scholars. If it is not, it will be

---

[3]   al-Bukhari, "Mazalim" 33; Muslim, "Iman" 242.
[4]   Ijtihad in Islamic Law is the process of deriving legal judgments from the unchanging, established principles of the Qur'an and the Sunna in order to deal with emerging circumstances. (Tr.)

regarded and rejected as an innovation that is contrary to Islam's jurisprudential principles.

- Human beings, created with an inherently noble disposition, pursue the truth. But sometimes they happen to find and embrace a falsehood. While searching for the truth, they sometimes are unintentionally taken in by misguidance and, thinking it to be the truth, mistake it for the truth.

- Many mirrors, each one more subtle than the other, reflect the Divine Power. They range from water to air, from air to ether, and thence to the World of Representations or Ideal Forms, and higher still to the World of Spirits and even to time and ideas. A word multiplies a million times in the mirror of air. The Pen of Divine Power accomplishes this in an amazing way. Things are reflected in these mirrors either with their apparent identities or with both identities and natures. Each reflection of a solid entity is a moving lifeless form; each reflection of a luminous spiritual entity is a living form connected to the original. Even if the reflection of a luminous entity is not identical to the original, it is not something different.

- Since the sun is shaken through its movement on its axis, its fruits (planets) do not fall. If it stopped shaking, its fruits would scatter.

- An idea is dark and spreads darkness unless illumined with the light of the heart. The white of the eye, which can be likened to the day, cannot engender sight until it is combined with the iris and pupil, which can be likened to night. In the same way, the "white portion" of an idea cannot engender sight of the truth unless combined with the heart's "iris and pupil."

- Knowledge without conviction is little better than ignorance. Siding with or adopting something is quite different from conviction.

- A fanciful, elaborate description of falsehood and decisive things misleads simple minds.

- A scholarly guide should be like a sheep, not like a female bird. A sheep gives its lamb her milk, whereas a female bird gives her chicks regurgitated food.

- A thing's existence depends upon the existence of all its parts. Since a thing's non-existence is possible through the non-existence of some of its parts, an impotent person tends to be destructive in order to demonstrate their power; they act negatively instead of acting positively.

- Principles of wisdom and laws of right have no effect upon ordinary people unless the former are combined with the law of the state and the latter with the rules of force.
- (In today's world) injustice or tyranny wears the cap of justice, treachery has donned the cloak of patriotic zeal, *jihad*[5] is called aggression and a violation of human rights, and enslavement has been called freedom. In short, opposites have exchanged forms.
- Politics based on personal interest is bestial.
- Showing love for a hungry wild animal only excites its appetite. Moreover, after it has fed upon you, it demands further payment for feeding upon you.
- Time demonstrates that Paradise is not cheap and that Hell is not futile.
- The merits of those considered "the elite" have led them to arrogance and oppression, whereas these merits should inspire them to modesty and self-effacement. Instead of arousing compassion and benevolence, the destitution of the poor and the poverty of common people have caused their abasement and servitude.
- If honor and merit result from a thing, it is offered to the elite and leaders. But if vice and evil proceed from it, it is divided and distributed among the common people.
- If people have no goals to pursue, or if the main objective is forgotten or neglected, the minds turn to individual egos and revolve around them.
- The origin of all revolutions, all corruption, and the cause and source of all vices and moral failings can be summed up in two short phrases: The first is: "I am full, so what is it to me if others die of hunger?" And the second is: "You will suffer so I may be comfortable. You will work so that I may eat." There is one single cure for the lethal poison of the first word that will cut it to the root: this is the *Zakah* enjoined and established by the Shari'a. The cure for the second disease is the prohibition of usury and interest. Qur'anic justice stands at the door of humanity and turns away usury and interest, proclaiming: "You

---

[5]   *Jihad* means striving in God's cause and for the good of humanity. (Tr.)

have no right to enter!" Yet humanity has ignored this prohibition and suffered a great blow.[6] It must heed it now to avoid receiving a greater one.[7]

- Wars between nations and states are being replaced by class war, for people do not want to be either slaves or wage-earners.

- One who follows an unlawful way (in Islam) for a lawful objective generally attains the opposite result of what they intended. The reward for an un-Islamic love, like that of (the second) Europe[8], is the Beloved's pitiless enmity.

- The past and all calamities should be considered in the light of Destiny. The future and sins committed should be referred to human free will and responsibility. This reconciles the extremes of *jabr* (fatalism) and *i'tizal* (denying Destiny's role in our actions).

- You should not seek solace in displaying impotence in what you can do or find a solution for, nor should you lament over what you cannot do or find a solution for.

- Wounds related to one's life can be healed, but wounds inflicted upon the dignity of Islam and the national honor are too deep to heal.

- Sometimes a single utterance drives an army to defeat, as a bullet may lead to the deaths of 30 million people.[9] Under the right conditions and circumstances, a (seemingly) insignificant act may cause its doer to be elevated to the highest of the high or reduced to the lowest of the low.

- A single truth can bring down a heap of lies. A single reality is preferable to a heap of fancies.

---

6   Said Nursi is referring to the First World War. (Tr.)

7   Unfortunately, humanity has not heeded this warning and has received another, greater blow, in the form of the Second World War. If humanity continues to ignore this warning, it will receive another, far greater one. (Tr.)

8   Said Nursi writes: "Europe is two. One is that which, benefiting from the religion of Jesus and Islamic civilization, serves human social life and justice through scientific and technological inventions, the other is that which is based on naturalistic and materialistic philosophy and, supposing the evils of civilization to be virtues, has driven humankind to vice and misguidance." For further discussion see , The Gleams, (Trans.), Tughra Books, New Jersey, 2008, pp. 161–168. (Tr.)

9   Gavrilo Princip, a Serbian private, assassinated Austro-Hungarian Archduke Francis Ferdinand and his wife; this was pretext for the outbreak of WWI, which resulted in 30 million deaths.

- You must always speak the truth, but it is not right to speak every truth.
- Those who attend the good side of everything contemplate the good. Those who contemplate the good enjoy life.
- People are energized by ambition and hope and are demoralized by hope's absence.
- From the time of its foundation, this Islamic State has seen itself as duty bound to sacrifice itself for the Islamic world and as the standard-bearer of the Caliphate; accordingly it undertook *jihad*, a collective religious obligation, to maintain Islamic independence and exalt the Word of God. The collapse of this state will be compensated for in the future with the Muslim world's happiness and independence, for its collapse is a calamity that urges us to develop brotherhood and sisterhood, which is the yeast or catalyst of our lives as Muslims.
- Here is a demonstration of how the wheel of time rotates in the opposite direction: They attribute to Christianity the virtues of civilization which are not its property, while Islam is accused of encouraging backwardness, something which Islam is opposed to and fights.
- A fine but tarnished diamond is always preferable to a piece of glass, no matter how well polished.
- The intelligence of those who seek everything in matter (material existence) is in their eyes; however, the physical eye is blind to what is spiritual.
- If a metaphor falls from the hand of knowledge to that of ignorance, it is transformed into fact and opens the door onto superstition.
- Seeing and showing someone or something as having more than what God has favored them with is essentially not doing them a favor. Therefore, it is much better to describe everything as it really is.
- Fame ascribes to the famous what they do not truly own.
- The Prophet's sayings are the mine of life and inspire truths.
- The revival of Islam means the revival of the nation. The life of Islam is the light of life.
- The Qur'an is a mercy for humanity, and urges a civilization that secures the greatest happiness for the most people.

    Western civilization, in its present phase, is established upon five negative principles: It is based upon might or force; the basic characteristic of force is aggression. It seeks to realize individual self-interest, which causes people to rush madly upon things to possess them. It considers life to be a struggle or conflict, the essential characteristic of which is contention and mutual repulsion. The basic bond it offers for the unity of people is racism or negative nationalism, which "feeds" by swallowing others, and engenders terrible conflict. Its enchanting service is to excite lusts and passions and facilitate the gratification of animal desires, which brutalize people.

As for the civilization which the Shari'a of Islam comprises and orders: it rests upon right, not might or force, and right requires justice and balance. Its goal is virtue, not self-interest, and virtue spurs mutual affection and love. Its principle of life is cooperation or mutual help instead of conflict, and this leads to unity and solidarity. Its means of unity between people are the ties of religion and citizenship, in place of racism and negative nationalism; and these lead to internal peace and brotherhood (and sisterhood), and urge only self-defense against external aggression. In place of lust and passion, the form of service of the Shari'a's civilization is guidance and the essential characteristic of guidance is progress and prosperity in a way that is befitting to humanity, and spiritual and moral perfection. Never break with Islam, for it guarantees our survival. Stick to it, heart and soul, or we will perish utterly.

- A general calamity is the consequence of a general failing of most people. Every calamity is the consequence of a failing, but at the same time it is also a door that opens to a means of reward for Muslims.
- Martyrs know that they are alive. Since they do not experience dying as death, they see that their lives, sacrificed for God's sake, are permanent, continual, and more refined.
- The pure, perfect justice of the Qur'an does not sacrifice the life of an innocent person even for the whole of humanity. In the sight of Divine Power and Justice, an individual's life is equal to the life of humanity. Yet some people can be so selfish that they would destroy everything and annihilate all of humanity, even the whole world if they could, if it seems to be an obstacle to the fulfillment of their desires.
- Timidity and weakness encourage external pressure and interference.
- Certain benefit should not be renounced for fear of potential harm.

- Politics is now a disease like the Spanish flu.

- Tell a mad person repeatedly, "You are well," and it is not unusual that they become cured. And tell a good one repeatedly, "You are bad," and it is not rare that they become bad.

- The enemy of the enemy is a friend as long as he remains an enemy, and the friend of the enemy is an enemy as long as he remains a friend.

- An obstinate one behaves in this way: if a devil helps or supports someone or their side, they hail them as "an angel" and calls down blessings upon them. But if they see an angel on the opposing side, they view this as a devil in the guise of an angel, and they call down curses on them.

- The cure for an ailment may be harmful to another condition. Excessive doses of any medicine can cause new illnesses.

- A society in which there is solidarity is an instrument that has been created to stir up the inactive, while a community in which there is malicious envy is an instrument created to pacify the active.

- If there is not healthy and sincere unity in a community, it will weaken as its numbers increase merely through population growth. This is like the multiplication of fractions. The amount grows less in proportion to how many times it has been multiplied.[10]

- Not affirming something's existence is often confused with affirming that it does not exist. The absence of evidence that something exists may justify people's not affirming its existence if they are not inclined to accept its existence. But affirming something's non-existence requires clear evidence to prove its non-existence, for not affirming its existence is doubt, while affirming its non-existence is denial.

- Even if doubt about one point of belief invalidates one, or even a hundred, proofs for it, its truth remains intact as there are thousands of other proofs supporting it.

---

[10]   Multiplying by or adding whole numbers leads to a greater number, whereas multiplying by fractions leads to a smaller number. Four times four makes sixteen. But when a third is multiplied by a third, the result is a ninth. In just the same way, if there is not a substantial, sincere unity in a community, its increase in number only causes it to become smaller, disintegrating and losing value.

- Follow the consensus of the majority of believers. The Umayyads did so and finally joined the Ahlu's-Sunna wa'l-Jama'a[11], although at first they were not careful in following the Religion. But since the Shi'a, who were careful and steadfast in adherence to the Religion in the beginning, preferred to remain a small minority, some among them eventually became *Rafidis*.[12]

- If there is consensus concerning what is good and true, and if seeking what is better and truer causes disagreement and discord, then what is true is truer than what is truer and what is good is better than what is better. So say: "My way is good and true," but never: "My way is the only way, the truest and best."

- Without Paradise, Hell's torment could not be perceived or understood.

- As time grows older, the Qur'an grows younger, and its secrets and signs become clearer and better understood. As light may be mistaken for fire, forceful eloquence may sometimes be mistaken for exaggeration.

- Degrees in heat occur through the existence of cold; the degrees of beauty occur through the existence of ugliness. God's Eternal Power is an essential Attribute of Divine Being and inherent in His Essence. This Power has no degrees, since impotence cannot access It. Thus, everything is equal before It.

- Consider: The sun's image in the sea and in its smallest wave or bubble has the same identity.

- Life, a manifestation of God's Oneness, brings unity to multiplicity.

- As long as who are the saints among people, which hour is most acceptable on Friday for prayer, the date of the Night of Power and Destiny during Ramadan, the Greatest Name among all God's Beautiful Names, and the appointed hour of death within a lifetime remain concealed and unknown, all remain esteemed and important. A life of twenty years with an unknown end is preferable to one of a thousand years with a known end.

---

[11] Ahlu's-Sunna wa'l-Jama'a is the overwhelming majority of Muslims who follow the way of the Prophet and His Companions in thought, creed, and action. (Tr.)

[12] The Rafidis are those Shi'is who accuse the overwhelming majority of the Prophet's Companions of apostasy because they did not elect 'Ali ibn Abi Talib, the 4th Caliph, as Caliph immediately after the Prophet, upon him be peace and blessings. (Tr.)

- The worldly recompense for evil is proof of punishment to come in the Hereafter.

- In the sight of Divine Power, provision or sustenance is as important as life. Provision is produced by Power, apportioned by Destiny, and nurtured by Grace or Favor. As life is the sure, certain outcome of particular circumstances and events, it is witnessed or visible in its totality. But provision is neither sure nor certain, for it is scattered and obtained over a certain time; it comes in uncertain degrees and leads people to contemplation. Those who appear to die of hunger before the sustenance stored in their bodies (as fat, for example) has been wholly consumed die from diseases caused by altering or abandoning routine nourishment.

- The licit sustenance of wild carnivores is innumerable animal carcasses. By eating them, these carnivores feed themselves and cleanse the earth's surface.

- Imagine that you have two pieces of food of equal nutritional value. One costs a hundred cents and the other costs ten dollars. If you prefer the latter solely for the few seconds of pleasure it will give your sense of taste, the inspector or doorkeeper of your body, then is this not the meanest form of waste?

- When pleasure calls, one should say, "It is as though I have eaten it (*Sanki yedim*)." One person who followed this principle could have eaten the equivalent of a mosque called *Sanki Yedim*, but he did not.[13]

- An easy life may be appealing when most Muslims are not hungry. But when most Muslims are hungry, no Muslim can choose such a life.

- Rather than welcoming transient pleasures with a smile, welcome transient ailments. Past pleasures lead one to regret, for "Alas!" indicates a hidden ailment. Past ailments lead one to sigh with relief, which gives news of a hidden joy and a favor that has come.

- Forgetfulness is also a bounty; it allows one to suffer the pains of only the present day; it makes one forget accumulated sorrows.

---

[13]   There is a mosque in Istanbul called *Sanki Yedim* (As If I Have Eaten It). Whenever the one who funded the building of this mosque wanted to eat something expensive, he would say, "It is as if I have eaten it," and saved the money he might have otherwise spent. He finally had a mosque built with the money which he saved in this way. (Tr.)

- Every calamity contains degrees of Divine Favor. Be mindful of the greater calamity, thereby being thankful for the favor of the lesser calamity. Concentrating on and exaggerating a calamity increases it, and this exaggerated reflection in the heart or imagination makes it real and troublesome.

- In social life, everyone has a window – status – through which to see and be seen. If the window is higher than their height (real stature or worth), they will, through pride, appear as tall (or taller). But if the window is lower than their height, they will bend and bow down out of modesty. In human beings, the measure of greatness is to know oneself as low-ranking or modesty, and the measure of true low-ranking is to feign greatness or conceit.

- Weak people's self-respect or dignity in the face of the strong or powerful is arrogance when assumed by the latter. Powerful people's modesty before weak people becomes self-abasement when assumed by the latter. In his office, the gravity of a person of authority is dignity, and his feeling of self-nothingness is self-abasement. But in his house, his feeling of self-nothingness is modesty, and his gravity, arrogance. Forbearance and sacrifice on one's own account are good and virtuous, but are bad and treacherous when done on behalf of others. People may bear patiently what has been done to them personally, but cannot bear patiently what is done to the nation on behalf of the nation. Pride and indignation on the nation's behalf are commendable, but are reprehensible on one's own behalf.

- Entrusting the accomplishment of an affair to God without taking all necessary measures and making all necessary arrangements is laziness. Leaving the realization of the desired outcome to God after having done all that can be done is to put trust in Him. Contentment with one's lot or the result after having exerted one's greatest efforts is praiseworthy contentment, and encourages further effort, reinvigorating one's energy and industry. However, contentment with what one already has is a deficiency and means lacking in necessary endeavor or efforts.

- Just as the commands of the Shari'a are obeyed or disobeyed, so too are the Divine laws of creation and life obeyed or disobeyed. The reward and punishment for the former is received mostly in the Hereafter, while the penalties and rewards of the latter are suffered mostly in this world. For example, the reward for patience is success, while the punishment for indolence is deprivation. The reward of labor is wealth, and the reward of steadfastness is triumph. Any claim to justice which is not egalitarian is a false claim.

- The same age and status or social standing cause rivalry and conflict. Being complementary and congruous is the basis of solidarity. An inferiority complex provokes arrogance. A weak character is the source of haughtiness. Impotence gives rise to opposition. Curiosity is the teacher of knowledge.

- The Power that created every thing with its own disposition has restrained humanity and animals through their need, in particular hunger, and put them in a certain order. It has also prevented disorder and confusion in the world and, by making need a motive for civilization, secured progress in every field.

- Boredom and distress are the teachers of dissipation; despair, misguidance in thought, and darkness in the heart are the mine of distress and depression.

- When men become womanish through focusing on worldly whims and fancies, women become masculine through crudity and impudence. If a beautiful woman enters a gathering of "brothers," ostentation, rivalry, and envy are aroused. Unveiling women and allowing them to mix freely with men to whom they are not related encourages vices or bad morals.

- Pictures, especially obscene ones, have an important part in people's present sinfulness and ill-temper.

- Statues, prohibited by Islam, are either petrified tyranny, or solidified passion, or embodied hypocrisy.

- The tendency toward expansion in a person who sincerely confirms and completely complies with the essentials and the basic injunctions of Islam is a tendency toward perfection. Yet the same tendency in another who is outside the sphere of obedience to Islamic essentials and who is indifferent to them is a tendency toward corruption and destruction. The right course of action during times of "storms" and "earthquakes" is not to open the door of *ijtihad* – that is to attempt to derive "new" laws from the Qur'an and Sunna; rather, it is to close the doors and shutter the windows (against innovation). Those who are heedless and indifferent in belief and the practice of the Religion should not be indulged with dispensations; they should rather be warned strictly and aroused with heavier responsibilities and greater care.

• Unprotected and misrepresented truths lose their value in valueless hands.

• Our earth resembles an animate being that displays signs of life. If it were reduced to the size of an egg, would it be a kind of animal? Or if a micro-organism were enlarged to the size of the earth, would it not resemble it? If the earth is living, then it must have a "soul." If the universe were reduced to the size of a person, with its stars forming the particles and atoms or elements of his/her constitution, would it not be a conscious, animate being? God has created many kinds of living entities like this.

• There are two kinds of Shari'a (Divine sets of laws): those issuing from the Divine Attribute of Speech that regulate humanity's (a microcosm) deeds and states, and those that issue from the Divine Attribute of Will and regulate the universe's (a macro-human) creation and operation. This second group is wrongly called nature. Angels constitute a mighty community; they convey, represent, and embody Divine Commands of creation and order which issue from the Divine Will and are known as the Shari'a of the creation and operation of the universe.

• When you compare the senses of a microscopic creature to those of a human being you are confronted by an astounding, mysterious truth: Each person is like *Suratu Ya-Sin*, and in each person *Suratu Ya-Sin* is inscribed.[14]

• Materialism is a spiritual plague; it has infected humanity with this terrible fever and made it subjected to the Divine Wrath and punishment. In proportion to the increase in humankind's ability to criticize and inculcate, this plague becomes more severe and spreads ever-wider.

• The most miserable, distressed, and wretched person is the one who is idle. For idleness is the nephew of non-existence, whereas exertion or working hard is the life of the body and the waking state of life.

---

[14]   *Suratu Ya-Sin* is the 36th chapter of the Qur'an. There are tablets on which the entire *Suratu Ya-Sin* are inscribed within the larger Arabic letters of Y(a) and S(in). (Tr.)

- The profit of banks, the doors of usury and its containers, is always for the worst of humankind – the infidels – and for the most unjust among the infidels, and for the most dissolute among the unjust. It is absolutely harmful to the world of Islam. The Shari'a does not require nor does it take responsibility for all humankind always being prosperous at all costs. For an infidel, particularly if they are at war with Islam and Muslims, does not deserve respect or legal protection.

- Friday sermons are to remind people of the essentials of Islam, not to expound upon its abstract theoretical points. Given this, the Arabic phrases expressing those essentials are the best suited for reminding in this way. When Qur'anic verses are compared even with the Prophet's sayings, it will be noticed that even the most eloquent one of humankind was unable to compete with the Qur'an's eloquence.

Part Two

Part Two

Gleams of Truth
Flowers from the Seeds of Truth
FROM BETWEEN THE CRESCENTS OF RAMADAN AND THE 'IYD DAY

This is a short *"Mathnawi"* on Islamic belief, thought, and action for students of the *Risale-i Nur*

NOTE: In both its composition and subject-matter, this collection is unlike other *mathnawis* or compilations of poetry. It bears the title *Lemeat* (Gleams of Truth) and was written in order to explicate, to some degree, the writer's previous work, *Hakikat Çekirdekleri* (Seeds of Truth); moreover, it is in prose form and does not contain entertaining images or unbalanced emotions. It was written as scholarly instruction for some of the students of Bediüzzaman, including his nephew, who was with him at the time of writing; in it are included the truths of the Qur'an and belief, entirely in accordance with logic. This is a lesson about the Qur'an and belief. As our master himself said, and as we can understand, Bediüzzaman had no predisposition to verse or poetry, and did not occupy himself with them.

Working for two or two and a half hours every day, Bediüzzaman wrote this work in versified form (though it was not poetry); the work was completed in twenty days during Ramadan. At that time, he was a member of the *Darü'l-Hikmeti'l-İslamiyye* ("The House of Islamic Wisdom"), and had numerous preoccupations. Although it was dictated "extempore" and completed very quickly, the work was not edited and was published as it was. In our opinion, it is a wonder, on account of its relation to the *Risale-i Nur*. No other compilation of poetry seems to be as remarkable as this one is, as easy to read as prose. God willing, this work will become a sort of *Mathnawi* for students of *Risale-i Nur*. It acts as a form of index for the *Risale-i Nur*, or a forerunner for it, as the *Risale-i Nur* appeared ten years later and was completed over twenty-three years.

The Risale-i Nur students,
Sungur, Mehmed Feyzi, Hüsrev

 REMINDER: AS THE SAYING GOES: "A PERSON IS HOSTILE TO WHAT they do not know." I have thought a great deal about poetry and rhyming simply because I do not know much about them. I have never wanted to change the reality of what I mean to fit into the demands of poetry. So, in this book, I have dressed sublime truths in an inelegant garment that is bereft of rhyme or meter.

In the first place, I do not know any better way and am only thinking of conveying the meaning. Secondly, I wanted to give form to my criticism of those poets who chisel the body to suit the clothes. Thirdly, a childish style such as this is preferable and more suited to occupy the carnal soul and heart during Ramadan. But, my reader, I must confess I have made a mistake and want to alert you to avoid making the same – do not be misled by the poor style into being carelessly disrespectful of its exalted truths!

AN EXCUSE: O Reader! I confess at the beginning that I have worried about my abilities in the art of writing and versification. As for verse and rhyme, I had never been able to produce even one poem. But suddenly I felt a desire to put things in verse, a desire which has persisted. There is an epic in Kurdish about the expeditions of the Companions called *Qawl-i Nawala Sisaban*. My spirit enjoyed its natural cadence, which is similar to a hymn. So I chose to use its verse form, but in a way particular to myself. I made a composition which somehow resembled verse, although I took no pains with the meter. Anyone who wishes may read it as easily as prose, without thinking of its verse-like form. Indeed, it would be better to consider it as prose so that the meaning can be better understood. The verses of each section are interrelated in respect of meaning. Readers should not ask about rhyming. A fez can be without a tassel, and meter can be without rhyme, verse without rules. I think that if a composition draws attention to itself through its artistry, the mind is preoccupied then with the art. Therefore, a composition is better when artless, thus not distracting attention away from the meaning.

My teacher in this work was the Qur'an, my book was life, and the one I addressed was myself. And you, my reader, are an eavesdropper. Eavesdroppers have no right to criticize; they must take what pleases them and ignore what they do not like. It is my hope that the readers' tongues will utter a prayer of forgiveness for me, or recite a *Fatiha*, God willing.

The Supplicant

I am a ruined grave, in which are piled up
Seventy-nine dead Saids with his sins and sorrows.
The eightieth is a gravestone for this grave;
All together they weep at the decline of Islam.
Together with my gravestone and the moaning grave of dead Saids
I advance toward my abode of tomorrow.
I am fully certain that the heavens and earth of the future
Will together surrender to Islam's clear, shining hand.
For its strength lies in its belief and blessings,
It affords peace and security to all beings.

Two supreme proofs of Divine Unity

With whatever is in it, the universe is a supreme proof; with its tongues of the unseen and manifest worlds, it declares God's Unity and glorifies Him. Announcing the Unity of the All-Merciful, it continuously proclaims:

There is no deity but He!

All the atoms of its cells, all its parts and members, are tongues mentioning God. Together they pronounce in that resounding voice:

There is no deity but He!

The tongues are infinitely various, the voices are of differing pitch, but they are united on one point – the mention of Him, saying:

There is no deity but He!

The universe is the macro-human; it mentions God in a loud voice, while all its elements and atoms add to that loud voice their tiny voices, declaring in unison:

There is no deity but He!

The universe is a circle of God's remembrance, reciting the Qur'an section by section. Its light comes from the Qur'an, and all beings with spirits reflect on the truth:

There is no deity but He!

The Qur'an, this Mighty, Glorious Criterion of Truth and Falsehood, is the most articulate proof of Divine Unity. All of its verses are truthful tongues, and rays from the lightning of belief. All together they declare:

There is no deity but He!

If you attach your ear to the bosom of that Criterion, in its profoundest depths you will hear clearly a heavenly voice which recites:

There is no deity but He!

Its voice is utterly exalted, utterly solemn, truly sincere, most friendly, utterly convincing, and equipped with proofs. Repeatedly it declares:

There is no deity but He!

All the six aspects of this proof of light are transparent: upon it is the flower and stamp of miraculousness and in it shines the light of guidance, which says:

There is no deity but He!

Beneath it lies subtly interwoven logic and proof; on its right the intelligence or reason is made speak and the mind completely affirms it, saying:

There is no deity but He!

On its left, identical to the right, the conscience is produced as a witness; before it lies pure good and its aim is happiness and prosperity, the key of which at every instant is:

There is no deity but He!

Its support beyond it, identical to "before it," is heavenly, pure Divine Revelation. All these six aspects are luminous and manifested in the sign of each is:

There is no deity but He!

Can any lurking suspicion, any conceivable, piercing doubt, any treacherous deviance sneak into that resplendent, shining castle with its lofty walls of *suras*, every word of which is an angel uttering:

There is no deity but He!?

The Qur'an of mighty stature is an ocean of Divine Unity. To take a single drop as an example from that ocean, look at only a single, slight

Nothing can exist without the existence of everything

Throughout the universe there is harmony and solidarity that is both concealed and observable – both in the inner and outer aspects of existence.

Both this solidarity and the cooperation – mutual assistance or reciprocal answering of needs – demonstrate that only an all-encompassing Power could do this: thus an atom is created and situated in a way appropriate for all its relations.

Every line and word of the book of the universe is animated; need urges them toward each other and acquaints them with each other.

Wherever it comes from, every call for help receives response: in the name of Divine Unity, all the surroundings are moved to help it in its need.

Every living word has a face that is turned and an eye that looks to all the sentences.

The sun's motion is for gravity and gravity provides the stability of the solar system

The sun is a fruit-bearing body; it shakes itself so that its fruit – which are mobile – do not fall.

If it were to stop moving and come to rest, then gravity would cease and its ecstatic followers would scatter through space and weep.

Small things are interconnected to larger things

Certainly, the one who has created the eye of a mosquito has created both the sun and the Milky Way.

And the one who has ordered the flea's stomach doubtlessly has set in order the solar system.

Also, the one who has given sight to the eye and need to the stomach has certainly adorned the eye of the sky with the kohl of light and spread a feast over the face of the earth.

There is a supreme miraculousness in the order of the universe

See, there is miraculousness in the organization of the universe; if to suppose the impossible all natural causes were agents that are able to do whatever they will,

They would, confessing their utter impotence in the face of this miraculousness, prostrate before it and declare: "*All-Glorified are You! We have no power! Our Lord, You are the Eternal, All-Powerful One of Majesty!*"

Everything is equal before the Divine Power

> Your creation and your resurrection are but as (the creation and resurrection of) a single soul. (31:28)

The Divine Power is essential to and inherent in the Divine Essence; impotence cannot access It.

There can be no degrees in Divine Power, nor can any impediment in any way obstruct It. Whether they be universal or particular, all things are the same in relation to It.

For everything is interconnected to and interdependent on everything else; one who cannot make everything can make nothing.

One who cannot hold the universe in his hand cannot create a particle

If one does not have a hand that is powerful enough to lift the earth, the suns, and the stars – those innumerable bodies – and string them in order like prayer-beads,

And place them on the head and breast of endless space, they cannot claim to create anything in the world; they have no right to claim to have invented anything.

Raising a species to life is the same as raising an individual to life

Just as revivifying a fly that has gone numb in the death-like sleep of winter is not difficult for the Divine Power,

Likewise, neither the death of the earth nor its resurrection will pose any difficulty for the Divine Power.

Nor will the raising to life of all beings with spirits present any greater problem.

Nature is Divine art

Nature is not the printer, it is something printed;

It is not the inscriber, but the inscription; it is not the doer or the agent, it is the recipient; it is not the source, but the pattern.

It is not the one who orders, it is the order; it is not the power, but the law; it is a set of laws that issue from the Divine Attribute of Will; it is not a reality that has a materialized self-existence.

The conscience recognizes God through its attraction

In the conscience there is an attraction, an infatuation; the conscience feels that it is constantly attracted by the pull of an attractive force.

If the All-Beautiful, Gracious One was to manifest Himself permanently without a veil, conscious beings would be overcome with ecstasy.

The consciousness – the human conscious nature – testifies decisively to a Necessarily Existent One, One of Majesty and Beauty and Grace;

The feeling of attraction is a testimony, and so too is the feeling of being attracted.

The innate disposition given by the Creator speaks the truth

A thing's innate disposition or God-given nature does not lie; whatever this innate disposition says is the truth. Given an inclination to grow, the tongue of the seed says: "I will sprout and yield fruit," and what it says is proven true.

The inclination toward life murmurs in the depths of the egg: "If God wills, I will be a chick." What it says is true.

If a handful of water intends to freeze inside an iron cannon-ball when it is cold enough,

The inclination to expand within it says: "Expand! I need more space." This command cannot be resisted.

Strong iron sets out to work, and does not prove it wrong; the water's truthfulness and honesty split the iron.

All these inclinations are Divine creational commands and each is a Divine decree. They are all Divine laws of creation and life, all manifestations of Will.

Divine Will directs all beings in this way: all inclinations conform to the commands of the Lord.

The Divine manifestation in the conscience is the same; the feeling of attraction and the feeling of being attracted are two pure "souls;"

They are two polished mirrors in which are reflected the eternal Beauty and the light of belief.

Prophethood is essential for humankind

The Divine Power, Which does not leave ants without a leader or bees without a queen

Surely would not leave humankind without a set of laws or a Prophet. The order of the universe self-evidently demands this.

The Ascension was for the angels what the splitting of the moon was for humankind

The angels saw in the Prophetic wonder of the Ascension a supreme saint-hood within the undeniable Prophethood.

That shining person mounted Buraq (carrying him to heaven) and was like lightning; like the traveling moon, he saw the world of light throughout.

In the same way for humanity, which is scattered through this visible world, *And the moon split* (54:1) was an important, observable miracle;

So for the dwellers in the world of spirits, the Ascension, pointed out in, *All-Glorified is He, He took His servant for a journey by night…* (17:1) was the greatest miracle.

The proof of the affirmation of faith is within it

The affirmation of faith contains two sentences, each of which testifies to the other; one is an argument and proof for the other.

The first is the a priori argument for the second, and the second is the a posteriori argument for the first.

Life is a manifestation of unity

Life is a light of unity through which unity is manifested in this realm of multiplicity. Truly, a manifestation of unity unifies multiplicity, thus making it a unified entity.

Life causes a single thing to own all things together, while for a life-less thing all things are non-existent.

The spirit is a law clothed in external existence

The spirit is a luminous law clothed in external existence and endowed with consciousness.

This spirit, which has a real, sensible existence, has become the brother, the companion, of that perceptible law.

Like established, constant natural laws, the spirit comes from the world of the Divine Command and the Attribute of Will.

The Power clothes it in a being with senses, attaches consciousness to its head, and makes an astral body the shell for that pearl.

If the Creator's Power were to clothe the laws operating in species in external existence, each would become a spirit;

If the spirit was stripped of external existence and consciousness, it would become an undying law.

Existence without life is like non-existence

Both light and life are the causes for beings to reveal themselves and be known. See, if there is no light of life,

Existence will be stained with non-existence; indeed, it is like non-existence. Even if it is the moon, it is a stranger and an orphan, unless it has life.

Thanks to life, an ant is greater than the earth

If you were to weigh an ant on the balance of existence, the universe to emerge from it could not be contained in our earth.

In my view, the earth is living. But if, according to what others suppose, you were to take the lifeless earth and place it in the other pan to the ant,

It would not amount to even half of the conscious head of the ant.

Christianity will follow Islam

Christianity will either become extinct or purified. It will surrender to Islam and give up arms.

It was fragmented repeatedly until finally Protestantism appeared, but it was unable to find there what was necessary to rectify it.

The veil was again rent, it fell into absolute misguidance. However, a part of it approached the affirmation of Divine Unity; in that it will find salvation.

It is preparing to be torn again. If it does not become extinct, Christianity will be purified and join Islam.

In this lies a mighty mystery to which the Pride of the Messengers alluded when he said: "Jesus will come and follow my Shari'a; he will be of my Community."

A partial or indirect view sees the impossible as possible

It is a well-known incident: a large group of people were scanning the horizon for the crescent moon to establish the beginning of the 'Iyd, but no one could see anything.

Then an aged old man swore that he had seen it. But what he had seen was a curved white eyelash.

The eyelash became his crescent moon. But how can a curved eyelash become the crescent moon? If you have understood our parable:

The motion of atoms has become the eyelash over your reason – a dark eyelash that blinds the materialist eye.

It cannot see the One Who has formed all species of beings, so misguidance comes upon you.

How can that motion replace the One Who has created and ordered the universe? It is a compounded impossibility to suppose the former to be the latter.

The Qur'an requires mirrors, not someone to act as a deputy

Rather than rational arguments, it is the sacredness of the source which encourages the mass of the Muslim Community and the common people to obey it and urges them to follow it.

Ninety per cent of the Shari'a is comprised of the obvious, indisputable matters and essentials of Religion, each of which is a diamond pillar.

The matters which are open to interpretation, controversial and secondary, only amount to ten per cent. One who has these ten gold pieces cannot own the ninety diamond pillars or put them in their purse, nor can they make them dependent on the gold pieces.

The source of the diamond pillars is the Qur'an and Hadith.[15] The pillars are their property and should always be sought in them.

---

[15]   The Hadith is the collection of Prophet Muhammad's words, actions, and the actions that he approved of in others. As the second source of Islam, the Hadith is identical to the concept of Sunna and are based on Revelation. When not capitalized, the word *hadith* refers

Books and interpretations of the Shari'a should be mirrors of the Qur'an or telescopes through which the Qur'an is examined. That sun of miraculous exposition does not need shadows or anyone to act on its behalf!

The falsifier of the truth adopts the false as true

Since by nature humans are noble, their purpose is to find the truth. However, sometimes falsehood comes to their hands, and supposing it to be the truth, they keep it in their breast pocket.

While digging out the truth, misguidance comes upon them involuntarily; supposing it to be the truth, they wear it on their head.

The mirrors of the Divine Power are numerous

The Power of the All-Majestic One has numerous mirrors. They open up windows, each more transparent and subtle than the other, all looking onto the World of Representations or Ideal Forms.

Various mirrors from water to air, air to ether, ether to representations or ideal forms, ideal forms to spirits, spirits to time, time to imagination, and from imagination to the mind, all represent the manifestations of God's acts. Turn your ear to the mirror of the air: a single word becomes millions!

The Pen of Power makes copies in an extraordinary way; this is the mystery of reproduction...

There are various sorts of representation

The image or reflection in a mirror is one of four sorts: it is either only the identity or the physical form of the thing reflected; or the identity together with the essential, living attributes; or both the identity and a ray from the thing's nature; or both the nature and the identity.

If you desire examples: a human being, the sun, the angel, and the word. The images of solid things in mirrors are moving dead forms.

The images of a luminous body in its reflections are living and connected to it; even if it is not the spirit itself or identical to it, they are none other than this.

---

to a single, specific word or action of the Prophet or the word or action he approved of in others. (Tr.)

They are each an expanded light. If the sun had been a living being, its heat would be its life, and its light, its consciousness – its image in the mirror has these qualities (i.e., it has both heat and light).

This explains the following mystery: Archangel Gabriel is both at the Lote-tree[16] and in the Prophet's Mosque in the form of Dihya[17] at the same instant – and who knows in how many other places!

Also, God knows how many places Azra'il can be present in simultaneously, taking the spirits of the dying.

At the same time, the Prophet appears to his Community both in the visions of the saints and in true dreams;

And on the Plain of the Supreme Gathering on Judgment Day he will meet with all to intercede on their behalf.

The "substitutes" (abdal) of saints appear and are seen in numerous places at the same instant.

One qualified to make ijtihad may deduce a new law for himself, but he cannot be a law-giver

Anyone who has the competence to practice ijtihad may deduce new laws for himself in matters about which there are no explicit verdicts in the Qur'an or Sunna; these are binding on that person, but not on others.

He cannot make laws and call on the Muslim Community to obey them. His conclusions are regarded as belonging to the Shari'a, but they cannot be included in the Shari'a as being binding on all Muslims. He may be a mujtahid, but he cannot be a law-giver.

It is only the consensus of the majority of scholars which bears the stamp of the Shari'a. The first condition for calling on others to accept an idea is acceptance by the majority.

Otherwise, such a call is innovation and must be rejected; it is kept in the throat, and must not be uttered!

---

16   The Lote-tree (Sidratu'l-Muntaha in the Qur'an, 53:14) of the furthest limit; it signifies the boundary between the realm of Divinity and the realm of creation. (Tr.)

17   Dihyatu'l-Kalbi was one of Prophet Muhammad's Companions. Archangel Gabriel sometimes came to the Prophet in his form. See, al-Bukhari, "Manaqib" 25; Muslim, "Iman" 271. (Tr.)

The light of reason comes from the heart

Unenlightened intellectuals should know this principle: an idea cannot be enlightened without the light of the heart.

As long as the ray of the mind has not been combined with the light of the heart, the result is darkness, oppression and ignorance. It is darkness dressed up in a false light.

Your eye has a white part, which resembles daytime, but it is blind and dark. But there is a pupil in it, which is dark like the night, but illuminated.

Without the pupil, that piece of flesh is not an eye, and you can see nothing. An eye without insight is also worth nothing.

So, if the dark pupil of the heart is not present in the white of thought, the contents of the mind will produce no knowledge or insight. There can be no reason or intellect without the heart.

The levels of knowledge in the mind are variable and can be confused

There are levels of knowledge in the mind that can be confused with one another and whose results are different. One first imagines something, then conceives of it, and clothes it in a form.

Afterwards, one reasons and reflects on this thing, then confirms it, and then has full conviction of it. Then they fully support it; then they become committed or devoted to it.

Your commitment is different, and so is your support, each of which results in a different state or attitude:

Steadfastness arises from commitment or devotion, while adherence comes from support or advocacy. Compliance proceeds from conviction and partiality from reasoning, while no ideas are formed at the level of conception.

If you remain at the level of imagination, the result will be sophistry. A beautiful, scenic description of falsehood and deceptive things will both injure and mislead simple minds.

Undigested knowledge should not be imparted to others

The true, scholarly guide is like a sheep, not a bird; they provide knowledge altruistically.

For the sheep gives its lamb digested food in the form of pure milk, whereas the bird gives its chick regurgitated food.

Destruction is easy, thus the weak are destructive

The existence of something depends on the existence of all its parts, while its non-existence is possible through the non-existence of one of its parts; thus, destruction is easy.

It is because of this that the impotent person never inclines to do or produce something positive or constructive that will show their power and capability; they act negatively, and are always destructive.

Force must serve right

If the principles of wisdom, laws of the state, precepts of right, and rules of force do not help or support one another,

They will neither be fruitful nor effective among the mass of the people. The marks or public symbols of the Shari'a will be neglected and fall into abeyance.

They will no longer be a point of support for people in their affairs, and people will no longer have confidence in or rely on them.

Sometimes opposites contain opposites

Sometimes opposites conceal their opposites within them. In the language of politics, the words are the opposites of their meanings.

Tyranny has donned the cap of justice. Treachery has found a cheap dress in patriotism. Jihad and war for God's sake have been labeled aggression and a violation of human rights. Enslavement to animal passions and the despotism of Satan have been called freedom.

Things have become their opposites, forms have been exchanged, names have been swapped, positions and ranks have changed places.

Politics based on self-interest is bestial

The politics of the present, which is based on self-interest, is a rapacious beast.

If you show love to a ravenous beast, you will not attract its compassion, but will rather sharpen its appetite.

Then it will turn on you and demand from you payment for the use of its claws and teeth.

Since human faculties have not been restricted in creation, their crimes are great

Unlike the animals, the faculties of human beings have not been restricted in creation; the good and evil that proceed from them know no limits.

If the selfishness that issues from one faculty and the egotism that proceeds from another are combined with haughtiness and obstinacy, such sins will be committed that no name has as of yet been found for them.

As these sins are proofs of the necessity of Hell, so too their penalty can only be Hell.

For example, in order to justify just one of his lies, a man desires, from his heart, the downfall of Islam.

The present time has shown that Hell is not unnecessary and Paradise is not cheap.

Sometimes good leads to evil

While in reality the merits of the elite should give rise to modesty and self-effacement in them, regrettably they have led to arrogance and oppression.

And while the destitution of the poor and the poverty of the common people should serve (as they do in reality) as means to arouse compassion and graciousness toward them, unfortunately they have now resulted in the abasement and servitude of the common people.

If honor and merit result from something, it is offered to the elite and leaders. But if vice and evil proceed from it, it is divided and distributed among the common people or employees and servants.

If a victorious tribe has won some honor, congratulations are offered to its Hasan Agha (the chief); but if some harm is obtained thenceforth, every curse is poured upon the members of the tribe. This is a sorry evil among humankind!

The absence of an objective strengthens egotism

If people have no goals to pursue, or if the main objective is forgotten or neglected, the minds turn to individual egos and revolve around them.

The ego thus becomes inflated, sometimes swelling with anger; it is not "pierced" or deflated so that it might become "we." Those who love themselves love no other.

A life of revolutions has sprung from the death of Zakah and a life of usury

The origin of all revolutions, all anarchy and corruption, the root and source of all evils, vices, and corrupt traits, can be summed up in two short phrases:

The first is: "I am full, so what is it to me if others die of hunger?" And the second: "You suffer so I may be comfortable. You work so that I may eat. Food is for me, laboring is for you."

There is one single cure for the lethal poison of the first word, which will sever it at the root and heal the situation:

That is the Zakah which is established by the Shari'a, a pillar of Islam. In the second word is a tree of Zaqqum[18]; what will uproot it is the prohibition of usury and interest.

If humankind desires salvation and loves its life, it must impose Zakah and abolish usury and interest.

If humankind prefers life, it must put to death usury of every sort

The bond of human relation that extends from the elite to the common people has been severed. So from below (the lower social strata) arise the cries of revolution, the shouts for revenge, the screams of grievance and envy.

From above descend fires of tyranny and scorn, the thunder of arrogance, and the lightning of oppression.

What should arise from below are love, respect, and accord. And from above should descend compassion and assistance, kindness and consideration.

If humankind desires these, it should hold fast to the Zakah and abandon usury and interest.

The Qur'anic justice stands at the door of the world, saying to usury and interest: "No entry! You have no right to enter!" They should retreat from this door and disappear from the world.

---

[18]   Zaqqum is an extremely bitter and thorny tree that grows at the bottom of Hellfire; the people of Hell will eat of it. (Tr.)

Humankind has not heeded this command and has thus received a severe blow; people should heed this call now before receiving another, more severe blow.

Humankind has demolished slavery; t will demolish wage-earning as well

In a dream I said the less severe wars between nations and states make way for fiercer wars between the social classes.

For in previous eras, humankind did not approve of slavery and crushed it with its blood. Now it has become a wage-earner; at the moment humanity is putting up with this burden, but this too will be crushed.

Humankind has grown old, having passed through four stages (of social progress): savagery, nomadism, slavery, and colonialism; now we are in the fifth age, that of wage-earning, but this too is passing.

An unlawful way leads to the opposite of what was intended

The murderer cannot inherit (from the one whom he has murdered); this is a very significant principle: "Someone who follows an unlawful way (in Islam) to reach his goal generally attains the opposite of what they intended in retribution."

Love of (the second) Europe is not a lawful love in view of the Shari'a; it is a blind imitation and disagreeable friendliness. Its consequence and recompense is the tyrannical hostility of the beloved and its crimes.

The sinner condemned to loss will find, in the end, neither pleasure nor salvation.

There is a grain of truth in both the Jabriyya and the Mu'tazila

O seeker after truth! The past and calamities, and the future and sins are not the same in the view and consideration of the Shari'a.

The past and calamities are considered from the perspective of Divine Destiny; for this, the fitting word is that of the Jabriyya, (who refer every event to Destiny).

Human accountability is taken into consideration about the future and sins; for this, the fitting word is that of the Mu'tazila, (who deny the role of Destiny in human actions). The Mu'tazila and Jabriyya are reconciled here.

There is a grain of truth in both of these false schools. Each has a particular situation; falsehood arises from a generalization that goes beyond a particular situation.

Only the incapable seek solace in impotence and complaints

If you want life, do not cling to impotence for things which have no solution;

If you want ease of mind, do not have recourse to regretful complaints about things for which there are no solutions.

If one on a rope fights with another on the ground, the one on the rope will lose

It is fitting for the abased to live in submissive peace with the infidels who war against Islam. The physical wounds heal, but the wounds to the dignity of Islam and the national honor are deep.

If an acrobat balancing on a rope offers to fight with someone standing on the ground, the latter will not refuse to engage, for the life of the acrobat and his amazing skill depend on his balance.

Once he loses his balance, see what will happen! The one on the ground, lacking any skill, has only to sit down or stand up.

An ambiguous proposition cannot be a universal one

An unconditioned proposition among the explicit statements of the Qur'an and Hadith is sometimes taken for a universal proposition.

Eventually the time comes when it is taken for a permanent rule. Its realization, even on one occasion in a single person is enough for it to be a truth.

For example, it is said, "An hour's sentry duty equals a year's worship." The Eskişehir and İnönü[19] fronts may have proven its truth.

The Qur'an states that one who kills an innocent person is considered to have killed the whole of humankind.[20]

---

[19]   Eskişehir and İnönü were fronts at which the Turkish army fought against the invading Greek army during the Turkish War of Independence. (Tr.)

[20]   The author is referring to the verse: ....*He who kills a soul unless it be (in legal punishment) for murder or for causing disorder and corruption on the earth will be as if he had killed all hu-*

A time comes when a single word brings about the defeat of an army. A single bullet led to the annihilation of thirty million people.[21]

Sometimes little things have greater outcomes

There are some circumstances in which a little action raises the performer of the action to the highest of the high;

Then there are circumstances where a slight action sends its doer to the lowest of the low...

For some people a moment is a year

Some innate capacities develop in an instant, while others are gradual, unfolding little by little. Human nature contains both of these.

They depend on conditions, and change accordingly. Sometimes they develop gradually. Sometimes they are like gunpowder – dark, suddenly exploding into glowing fire.

Sometimes a look transforms coals into diamonds. Sometimes a touch can change a stone into elixir.

A single look from the Prophet transformed an ignorant nomad into an enlightened one of knowledge in an instant.

If you want a comparison: 'Umar before Islam, and 'Umar after Islam.

Compare the two: a seed and a tree. The seed instantaneously produced fruit. That look of Muhammad, the grace of the Prophet, upon him be peace and blessings,

Suddenly transformed the coal-like natures in the Arabian Peninsula into diamonds. He enlightened characters that were as black as gunpowder; they all became shining lights.

A lie is a word of unbelief

One grain of truth burns a million lies. A grain of reality destroys a castle of dreams. Truthfulness is a supreme principle, a shining jewel.

If speaking the truth may cause harm, silence can be preferred; but there is never a place for lies, even if they appear to have some use.

---

mankind; and he who saves a life will be as if he had saved the lives of all humankind.... (5:32)
[21]   See footnote 9.

Whatever you say must be true, whatever judgment you give must be right, but you have no right to voice all that is true.

One should be well aware of this, and adopt it as one's principle: "Take what is clear and untroubled, leave what is turbid and distressing."

See the good side of things, so that you will have good thoughts. Know things to be good and think of them as good, so that you will find pleasure in life.

In life, hope and thinking well of things is life itself, while despair and thinking ill of others is the destroyer of happiness and killer of life.

In an assembly in the World of Representations or Ideal Forms

Comparisons between the Shari'a and modern civilization, and between scientific genius and the guidance of the Shari'a

In a true dream on a Friday night at the beginning of the period of truce following World War I, I was asked by a supreme assembly in the World of Representations and Ideal Forms:

"What will emerge in the Muslim world following the defeat?" I replied, as the representative of the present age, and they listened to me:

From the times of its foundation, this State saw itself as duty-bound to sacrifice itself for the Islamic world and as the standard-bearer of the Caliphate,

And accordingly it undertook *jihad*, a collective religious obligation, to maintain Islamic independence and exalt the Word of God.

Over time, the calamity that has struck this State, this Muslim nation, will certainly bring prosperity and freedom to the Muslim world.

This present disaster will be compensated for in the future. One who loses three and gains three hundred in return makes no loss. As a zealous laborer, they change their present for a better future.

For this calamity has aroused compassion and Islamic solidarity and brotherhood, the yeast or catalyst of our lives, to an extraordinary degree; it has given a wonderful impetus to our brotherhood.

The present civilization, which is in fact meanness, will change form, and its system will be demolished; it is then that an Islamic civilization will emerge. Muslims will certainly be the first to enter it voluntarily.

PART TWO / GLEAMS OF TRUTH   43

If you want a comparison between the civilization of the Shari'a and the present one, closely examine the principles of each and consider their consequences:

The principles of present-day civilization are negative. Its foundations and values are five negative principles. Its machinery is based on these.

Its point of support and reliance is might or force rather than right, and the basic characteristic of force is aggression and hostility, from which treachery arises.

Its goal is, instead of virtue, the gratification of mean self-interest, the essential characteristic of which is conflict and rivalry, and the consequence of which is crime.

Its law of life is conflict rather than cooperation and mutual helping; the essential characteristic of conflict is contention and mutual repulsion; the consequence is poverty.

Its basic bond between peoples is racism or racial discrimination, which develops to the detriment of others; it is nourished and strengthened by the right of others being devoured.

Negative nationalism or racism paves the way for constant, terrible clashes, disastrous collisions; the result is destruction.

The fifth is this: the enchanting service of the present civilization excites lusts and passions, facilitating the gratification of animal desires; the consequence is dissipation.

The basic characteristic of lusts and passions is always this: they transform humans into beasts, changing their character; they deform them, perverting their humanity.

Most of these civilized people – if you were to turn them inside out – would appear as apes and foxes, snakes, bears, and swine. Their characters have appointed their forms. They appear to the imagination in their furs and skins!

By contrast, the Shari'a, is the balance of the earth. The mercy in the Shari'a comes from the heaven of the Qur'an. The principles of the Qur'anic civilization are positive. Its mechanism for happiness turns on five positive principles:

Its point of support and reliance is right instead of might and the unchanging characteristic of right is justice and balance, which give rise to salvation, security and well-being, removing wretchedness and villainy.

Its aim is virtue instead of self-interest and the basic character of virtue is love and mutual attraction. Happiness arises from these, and enmity disappears.

Its principle in life is cooperation instead of conflict and killing, and the essential characteristic of cooperation is unity and solidarity; these enliven the community.

In place of lust and passion, its form of service is guidance and the essential characteristic of guidance is progress and prosperity in a way that is befitting to humanity, as well as enlightenment and perfection in a way that is required by the spirit.

While racism and negative nationalism destroy the point of unity among the masses, the bonds the Shari'a establishes between peoples are those of religion, citizenship, profession, and the brotherhood of belief.

The basic characteristics of these bonds are sincere brother/sisterhood, and general salvation, security and well-being. The Shari'a only demands self-defense in the case of external attacks.

Now you have understood why Muslims have remained distant from the present civilization without adopting it.

Up to the present, Muslims have not entered this present civilization voluntarily, it has not suited them; rather, on them have been clamped the fetters of bondage.

While it should have been the cure for humankind, this civilization has become the poison. It has cast eighty per cent of the population into destitution and misery and given false happiness to ten per cent.

The remaining ten per cent has been left uneasy, stranded between the two. The profits that come from trade have gone to the tyrannical minority. But true happiness is the happiness shared by all, or at least salvation for the majority. The Qur'an, revealed as a mercy for humankind, only accepts civilization of the kind

That brings happiness to all, or at least to the majority. In the present civilization, passions are unrestricted, impulses and fancies too are free; this is an animal freedom.

Passions dominate people, impulses and fancies too are despotic; they have made unnecessary needs essential ones, and banished ease and relief.

While in primitive life a person was in need of four things, civilization has made them needy of a hundred, and impoverished them.

Lawful labor is insufficient to meet the cost. This has driven humanity towards fraud and the unlawful. It is due to this that civilization has corrupted the essence of morality.

It has given certain wealth and glitter to society and the human species, but it has made the individual immoral and indigent. There are numerous testimonies to this.

All of the savagery and crimes in former times and all the cruelty and treachery have been vomited by this malignant civilization all at once, and its stomach is still retching.[22]

The fact that the Islamic world is able to remain aloof is both meaningful and noteworthy. It has been reluctant to accept this civilization, and has acted coldly.

Truly, the distinguishing quality of the Divine light in the illustrious Shari'a is independence and self-sufficiency.

It is due to this quality that the light of guidance has never allowed the genius of Rome, the spirit of (European) civilization, to dominate it.

The guidance of the Shari'a cannot be combined with the philosophy of the latter, nor be grafted onto it, nor follow it.

The compassion and the dignity of belief to be found in the spirit of Islam, and the truths of the Shari'a which it has nourished – the Qur'an of miraculous exposition has been taken the truths of the Shari'a in its shining hand;

Each of these truths of the Shari'a is a Staff of Moses in that shining hand. In the future that sorcerer civilization will prostrate in wonderment before it.

Now, note this: there were two geniuses – Ancient Greece and Rome, those twins from a single stock. One was imaginative, the other materialist.

Like water and oil, they never combined. Such a phenomenon required time, civilization strove to do so and Christianity tried, but none has been able to combine them.

---

22   That is, the civilization will vomit more terribly. It has vomited in the form of the two world wars in such a fashion that it has soiled the air, ground, and sea, staining them with blood.

Both preserved their partial independence. They have remained as if two spirits (in a single body); now they have changed their bodies; one has become German, the other French.

They have experienced a sort of reincarnation. O my dream-brother! This is what time has shown. Those twin geniuses have rejected any moves to combine them;

They are still not reconciled. Since they are twins, they are brothers and friends, companions in progress; but they have fought and never made peace.

How could it therefore be that the light of the Qur'an and the guidance of the Shari'a, when it has a completely different source, origin, and place of appearance, is reconciled with the genius of Rome, the spirit of modern civilization, and should join and combine with it?

That genius and this guidance – their origins are different: guidance descends from the heavens, genius emerges from the earth. Guidance works in the heart and genius works in the mind.

Genius works in the mind and confuses the heart. Guidance illuminates the spirit, making its seeds sprout and flourish; dark human nature is illuminated by it.

The capacity of guidance for perfection suddenly advances; it makes the carnal soul a docile servant; it gives zealous and endeavoring humans an angelic countenance.

As for genius, it focuses its attention primarily on the carnal soul and physical being; it comes into nature, making the soul an arable field and the carnal potentials develop and flourish;

It subjugates the spirit, causing the seeds to dry up; it displays satanic features in humankind. But guidance gives happiness to both lives – this and the next – and spreads light in both this world and the next, elevating humankind.

Genius, like Antichrist blind in one eye, sees only this life and this world; it is materialist and world-adoring. It turns humans into beasts.

Genius worships deaf nature and serves blind force. But guidance recognizes the conscious Art (manifested as nature) and turns to the wise Power (that gives existence to nature). Genius draws a veil of ingratitude over the earth while guidance scatters the light of thanks.

It is because of this that genius is deaf and blind, while guidance is hearing and seeing. In the view of genius, the bounties of the earth are ownerless booty;

It prompts the desire to usurp and steal them thanklessly, to savagely snap them off from nature.

In the view of guidance, the bounties scattered over the breast of the earth and the face of the universe are the fruits of Mercy; it sees a gracious hand beneath every bounty, and has kissed it in gratitude.

I cannot deny that there are numerous virtues in civilization, but they are neither the property of Christianity, nor the invention of Europe.

Nor are they the product of this century; they are the common property of humanity, produced as the result of the conjunction of thoughts and studies over time, from the laws of the revealed religions, and emerge out of innate need,

And particularly from the Islamic revolution brought about by the Shari'a of Muhammad. No one can claim ownership of these.

> The leader of the assembly from the World of Representations asked another question:

QUESTION: "Calamities are always the result of treachery but pave the way for reward. O man of the present century! Divine Destiny has dealt a blow and Divine Decree has passed sentence.

"What did you do so that both the Divine Decree and Destiny have so judged you – that the Divine Decree has sentenced you to this calamity and given you a beating?

"It is always the error of the majority which causes general disasters."

I said in reply:

ANSWER: Humankind's misguided thinking, Nimrod-like obstinacy, Pharaoh-like haughtiness grew and grew on the earth until they reached the heavens. Humanity also offended the sensitive mystery of creation.

It caused the shudders of the last war to pour down from the heavens like the plague and deluge; it caused a heavenly blow to be dealt to the infidel.

This means, the calamity was the calamity of all humankind. The common cause, inclusive of all humankind, was the misguided thinking that arose from materialism – bestial freedom, the despotism of carnal desires and fancies.

Our share in it resulted from our neglect and abandonment of the pillars of Islam. For the Creator the All-Exalted wanted one hour out of the twenty-four.

He ordered us, willed that we, for our good, assign one hour for the five daily Prayers. But out of laziness we gave them up, neglected them in heedlessness.

So we received the following punishment: He made us perform Prayers of a sort during these last five years through a constant, twenty-four hour drill and hardship, keeping us ceaselessly moving and striving.

He also demanded of us one month a year for fasting, but we pitied our carnal souls, so in atonement He compelled us to fast for five years.

He wanted us to pay as *Zakah* either a fortieth or a tenth of the property He gave us, but out of miserliness we did wrong: we mixed the unlawful with our property, and did not give the *Zakah* voluntarily.

So He had our accumulated *Zakah* taken from us, and saved us from what was unlawful in our property. The deed causes the punishment of its kind. The punishment is of the same as the deed.[23]

Good, righteous acts are of two sorts: one positive and voluntary, the other negative and enforced. All pains and calamities are good deeds, but they are negative and enforced. The *hadith* that tells us of this[24] offers consolation.

---

[23]   I did not mention the *Hajj* in the dream, for neglect of the *Hajj* and its wisdom drew not calamity, but Divine Wrath, and the punishment it incurred was not atonement for our sins but an increase in our sins. It was the neglect of the elevated Islamic policy, which exists in the *Hajj* and brings unity of views through mutual acquaintance and cooperation through mutual assistance, and it was neglect of the vast social benefits contained in the *Hajj* which have prepared the ground for the enemy to employ millions of Muslims against Islam. Those were Indian Muslims! Thinking that he was their enemy, they killed their father (the Ottoman State), and now they are weeping beside his dead body. There are the Tatars and the Caucasian peoples! They understood that the one in whose killing they had collaborated with the enemy was their poor mother, but it was too late! They are weeping at her feet. These are the Arabs! They mistakenly killed their heroic brother, and now in their bewilderment they do not even know how to weep. These are the Africans! They killed their brother unknowingly, now they are lamenting. This is the Muslim world; it heedlessly helped the enemy kill its standard-bearing son, now it is pulling its hair out, groaning and lamenting. Instead of hastening to the *Hajj* eagerly, which is pure good, millions of Muslims have been made to make long journeys under the enemy flag, which is pure evil. Ponder on this and take heed!

[24]   The Pride of humankind says: "In whatever circumstance a believer is, it is to his good. This is not so for anyone other than believers. For if something happy happens to him, he

This sinful nation has made its ablutions in blood; it has repented with deeds. As an immediate reward, four million, a fifth of this nation, were raised to the degree of sainthood through the rank of martyrdom or warring for God's sake; this wiped out their sin.

The elevated assembly from the World of Representations appreciated these words.

I woke up suddenly; rather, this was a meeting in true wakefulness before I went to sleep. In my view, wakefulness is a dream and a dream is a sort of wakefulness.

There I was the representative of this age, and here I am Said Nursi!

Rust-covered guidance is still a diamond

The guidance of Islam has rusted, while the genius of the present civilization has been gilded with desires and passions.

Even if a peerless diamond has rusted, it is always preferable to a gilded piece of glass. That diamond has been engraved with a heavenly inscription; the eyes of materialists do not see that peerless inscription; nor can they read it.

Materialists seek everything in matter; their intelligence is in their eyes, they are blind to whatever is spiritual, for bodily eyes are blind to that.

Ignorance takes a metaphor for a fact

If a metaphor falls from the hand of knowledge to that of ignorance, it is transformed into fact, and opens the door onto superstition.

During my childhood I saw an eclipse of the moon. I asked my mother, and she said: "A snake has swallowed it." I asked her: "Why is it visible, then?" She said: "The snakes there are semi-transparent."

A metaphor like this is perceived as a reality: At a Divine command, with the earth interposing between the points of intersection of the orbit of the moon and the sun, known as "the head" and "the tail," the moon is eclipsed.

---

thanks God, and this is to his good. If some harm touches him, he remains patient, and this also is to his good." (*Muslim*, "Zuhd" 64; *ad-Darimi*, "Riqaq" 61.) (Tr.)

The two hypothetical arcs that are formed and resemble two snakes were called *"Tinninayn* (two snakes)." The name was invented to explain an astronomical event figuratively and came to be taken to be in reality that with which it had been compared.

Exaggeration is implicit denigration

Whatever you describe, describe it as it really is. In my view, exaggerated praise is implicit denigration.

Seeing and showing someone or something as having more than what God has favored them with is, essentially, not a favor to them.

Fame is oppressive

Fame is a despot; it ascribes the property of others to the famous.

Of the witticisms attributed to the famous Nasreddin Hoja[25], only its *zakah*, that is, one-fortieth or at best one-tenth, can belong to him.

The imaginary renown of Rustam-i Sistani plundered an age of the glories of Iran.

His legendary image plundered the heroism of others, and was combined with superstition, thus carrying Rustam-i Sistani beyond the limits of humanity.

Those who suppose the Religion and life to be separable are the cause of disaster

The mistake of the Young Turks[26] was that they did not know that our Religion is the basis of our life; they thought the nation and Islam were different from one another.

They imagined the present civilization would endure and dominate, and saw the happiness of life and prosperity as lying within it.

---

[25]   Molla Nasraddin or Nasreddin Hoja was a thirteenth-century Muslim figure who was famous and remembered for his wisdom, legendary wit, funny stories and anecdotes. (Tr.)

[26]   The Young Turks were biased toward modern Western currents of thought and against the Ottoman administration. They struggled particularly against the government of Sultan Abdulhamid II. (Tr.)

Now time has shown us that the system of civilization is corrupt and harmful[27]; unequivocal experience has taught us this:

The Religion is the very life of life, its light and its foundation. The revival of this nation is possible only through the revival of the Religion. Muslims have understood this.

In contrast to other cultures, our nation is able to progress to the extent that we adhere to our Religion. It has declined to the degree we neglected it.

This is a historical fact, which we have pretended to forget.

Death is not as terrifying as imagined

It is an incorrect, misguided supposition that makes death terrifying. Death is a change of clothes, or a change of places. It leads from the dungeon to garden.

Whoever desires life should desire martyrdom. The Qur'an tells us that the martyrs are living. Martyrs, who do not experience the pangs of death, know and see themselves to be alive.[28]

But they find their new lives to be purer. They do not suppose that they have died. Note carefully the difference between them and the dead; it is as the following:

In a dream two persons are walking in a beautiful garden where there is every sort of delight. One knows it is only a dream and receives no pleasure from this.

It gives him no contentment; rather it fills him with regret. However, the other one knows that they are awake, and experiences true joy; this is real for them.

---

27   This refers to the oppressive, anti-religious civilization, which is moving towards its demise.

28   The Qur'an declares: *And say not of those who are killed in God's cause: "They are dead." Rather they are alive, but you are not aware* (2:154). *Do not think at all of those killed in God's cause as dead. Rather, they are alive; with their Lord they have their sustenance, rejoicing in what God has granted them out of His bounty, and joyful in the glad tidings for those left behind who have not yet joined them, that (in the event of martyrdom) they will have no fear, nor will they grieve. They are joyful in the glad tidings of God's blessing and bounty (that He has prepared for the martyrs), and in (the promise) that God never leaves to waste the reward of the believers.* (3:169–171). (Tr.)

The dream is the shadow of the World of Representations, which is the shadow of the Intermediate Realm. It is due to this that their principles are like one another.

Politics is diabolical in people's minds; one should seek refuge in God from this

Modern politics sacrifices the minority for the comfort of the majority. Worse than this, the despotic minority sacrifices the majority of people for itself.

Qur'anic justice never sees the life of a single innocent person as being expendable; it never allows an individual's blood to be spilled, even for all humankind, let alone for the majority in a particular jurisdiction.

The verse, *He who kills a person unless it be (in legal punishment) for murder... will be as if he had killed all humankind* (5:32), lays two mighty principles before our eyes.

One is pure justice. This sublime principle is that just as the individual and the community are equal in relation to the Divine Power, the Divine Justice also sees no difference between them.

This is a permanent, established Divine and Prophetic principle and practice. An individual may sacrifice their rights themselves, but the law cannot sacrifice them, not even for all humankind.

The canceling of one's rights, or the spilling of one's blood, or the annulment of one's innocence is equal to the canceling of the rights of all of humanity, or the annulment of the innocence of all of humankind.

The second principle is this: if a self-centered person can murder an innocent person out of greed or passion, he may destroy the whole world if capable of that, should it be an obstacle to the fulfillment of his desires, and annihilate all humanity.

Weakness emboldens the enemy; God may try His servants, but they cannot try Him

O fearful, weak one! Your fear and weakness are futile and harmful to you; they embolden external influences and draw them toward you.

O you who suffer from doubts and delusions! A sure benefit should not be renounced for fear of potential harm. What you need is to take action; the outcome is with God.

One cannot interfere in God's concerns. He takes His servant to the arena of trial and says: "If you do that, I'll do this."

But the servant can never try God. If he says, "Should God give me success, I'll do this," he is transgressing his limits.

Satan said to Jesus: "Since it is He Who does everything, and His Destiny does not change, then throw yourself down off the mountain, and see what He will do with you."

Jesus replied: "O accursed one! God's servants cannot put Him to the test!"[29]

Islamic politics should proceed from Islam;
politics should not be instrumental for others.
partisanship causes hearts to be divided, not united

The politics of Istanbul at the present time resembles the Spanish flu, infecting people; indeed, it sometimes causes delirium.

Political madness is the product of a Byzantine (i.e. deceitful and clandestine) mindset; politics does not go round and round by itself; rather it does so by means of an external orientation.

Europe hypnotizes politics and whispers in its ears. Thus, one can say a play is being staged here.

As the whisper comes from outside, if it is negative, it has, like individual letters, no value in itself; it is only beneficial when combined with others.

Our free will no longer has a part in it, so even if we are well-intentioned, our good intentions are of no use.

If the external whisper is positive, its value, like words in a sentence, is first for itself, and then, indirectly, for others.

The political divergences here go in opposite directions, and they have no point of intersection in the country; it is not possible for them to come together anywhere on the entire face of the wide earth.

Since this is so, those who take a positive, constructive way should be educated and follow knowledge. As the weak ones or the minority cannot guard the Qur'an, the powerful hand or the majority should guard it.

---

[29]   Ibnu'l-Jawzi, *Talbisu Iblis*, 344.

They should love and adhere to it, for the Religion cannot be used negatively or for a negative result. The 31-March Event[30] showed this.

It showed that even the least negative use of the Religion in the homeland yields a terrible result. Muslims came out of this as losers.

Do not overdo those things you like

The cure for one ailment may be harmful to another; what is an antidote for one becomes poison for another. If the cure is taken to excess, it causes illness and becomes fatal.

The eye of obstinacy perceives an angel as a devil

Obstinacy causes one to behave in this way: if a devil helps or supports one or their side, they hail them as "an angel" and call down blessings upon them.

But if they see an angel on the opposing side, they view them as a devil in the guise of an angel, and they call down curses on them out of enmity.

You sometimes receive help from places you did not expect

It is not rare that a mad person recovers when people repeatedly suggest to him that he is well, while a good person becomes bad when people repeatedly accuse them of badness.

Thus, the enemy of the enemy is a friend so long as they remain an enemy, and the friend of the enemy is an enemy so long as they remain a friend.

The Ape became a friend and helped, why should the Bear not do so? A swine strangles you, and a bear strangles it and becomes a friend to you.

Never prod at this bear or cause it to attack you. When you are burning in a fire, a great flood will come to extinguish you, thus becoming a friend for you.

Just as you did not become an ape (by receiving its help), so too you will not become a bear (by being friendly with it).

---

[30]   The 31 March Event was a revolt which broke out on April 13, 1909 in Istanbul. Its real nature and reasons have not yet been revealed. It resulted in the dethroning of Sultan Abdulhamid II and the coming into power of the Unity and Progress Party. (Tr.)

The catalyst of the life of a community is sound and sincere solidarity

A society in which there is solidarity is an instrument that has been created to stir up the inactive; while a community in which there is malicious
envy is an instrument created to pacify the active.

If there is not a sound or sincere unity in a community, it will weaken
as its numbers increase through mere population growth. It is like the multiplication of fractions. The number grows less in proportion to how many
times they have been multiplied.

Even if non-acceptance is your right, refutation is not

O seeker after truth! If something is related to you (particularly concerning
a truth of belief or in the form of a *hadith* (Prophetic Tradition),

What falls upon you is to accept it, if there is a proof for its accuracy.
If there is not, you may avoid its acceptance, which is a doubt.

The non-existence of a proof is an argument for your non-acceptance
of it, whereas your claim of its non-existence means refutation and denial,
which requires proof.

Something which cannot be established with proof cannot be claimed
to be non-existent without proof.

Non-acceptance of something's existence is usually confused with the
acceptance of its non-existence, though one is doubt and the other, denial.
You have no right to denial.

It sometimes happens that there are many phrases related to the same
incident and which are intended to convey the same meaning, or the meaning is something that has numerous indications or arguments.

If one or even ten of these are doubted or refuted, the existence of the
narration and the intended meaning cannot thereby be refuted.

One should follow the majority of Muslims

O seeker after salvation and security! A *hadith* indicates that we should follow and keep the company of the majority of Muslims.[31]

---

31   *Muslim*, "'Imara" 59; *at-Tirmidhi*, "Fitan" 7; *Abu Dawud*, "Salah" 46.

The Umayyads were, in the beginning, not careful to follow the Religion, but after they joined the majority of the Muslim Community, they were eventually included among the Ahlu's-Sunna wa'l-Jama'a.

The Shi'a were careful and steadfast in adherence to the Religion in the beginning, but a portion of them who were in the minority eventually formed the sect of Rafidis.

This is a significant, noteworthy reality.

After finding what is right, do not cause discord for the sake of something better

O seeker after truth! If there is consensus concerning what is good and true, and seeking what is better and truer causes disagreement and discord, then what is true is truer than what is truer, and what is good is better than what is better.

Islam is peace and reconciliation; It wants no dispute or hostility within

O World of Islam! Your life lies in unity, and if you want unity, your guiding principle should be the following:

You should adopt the principle, "This is true," rather than "This alone is true;" and "This is the best," rather than "This is what is exclusively good."

Every Muslim should say about their own school and way: "This is true; I do not interfere with others. Even if the others are good too, mine is the best."

They should not say: "This alone is true, the others are all false. Only mine is good, the others are all wrong and unpleasant."

The mindset of exclusiveness arises from self-love. It eventually becomes a disease and leads to dispute.

If the existence of numerous ills and cures is a rightful reality, right will also multiply. The variation of needs and foods is right, and right becomes diverse.

The multiplication of capacities and education is right, and this right will also multiply. A single substance is both poison and the antidote.

The truth is not fixed in the secondary matters of the Religion; it is relative and compounded according to the differences of temperament and circumstance.

The temperaments of those responsible for the conduct of such matters have a share in them, and they are concluded and formed accordingly.

The founders of the schools of law made judgments in non-specific terms, leaving the specification of the limits of their schools to the various temperaments that followed.

Bigoted attachment to a school causes the rulings of that school to be generalized, and partisanship arising from this leads to dispute.

The deep rifts between the classes of humanity before Islam, and the great distance between peoples and places demanded the existence of numerous Prophets at any one time, and a variety of Shari'as, and numerous sects.

Islam caused a revolution among humankind, and peoples drew closer to each other. The different Shari'as were summed up in a single Shari'a, and there was one Prophet.

But the levels of humankind were not the same, so the schools of law multiplied. If a single system of training and education were sufficient and proper for all, then the schools could unite.

There is great wisdom in the creation and combination of opposites:
the sun and a minute particle are equal in the hand of Power

O brother with an alert heart! The Power manifests Itself in the combining of opposites. There is pain in pleasure, evil within good, ugliness within beauty, harm within benefit, trouble within bounties, fire within light... do you know why this is so?

It is thus, so that relative truths may be established and so there may be many things within a single thing, and numerous various incidents of existence become apparent.

Swift motion makes a point look like a line. The speed of spinning makes a point of light look like a luminous circle.

There must be relative truths so that seeds may sprout in this world. These constitute the clay of the universe, the bonds of its order, the connections among its inscriptions. These relative realities will become truths in the Hereafter.

The degrees of heat are due to the existence of cold. The degrees of beauty come about through the intervention of ugliness. The apparent cause becomes as if the ultimate cause or raison d'être.

Light is indebted to darkness, pleasure is indebted to pain; there is no consciousness of health without illness.

If there was no Paradise, perhaps Hell would not be torment. Hell cannot exist without extreme cold. If there were no extreme cold (besides its heat), Hell would not burn.

The Ever-Living Creator has demonstrated His Wisdom in the creation of opposites and His Majesty has become apparent.

That Everlasting All-Powerful One has displayed His Power in the combining of opposites, and His Grandeur has become manifest.

However, since the Divine Power is essential to and inherent in the Divine Essence, It can comprise no opposites and therefore impotence cannot intervene in It; there can be no degrees in It; nothing can be difficult for it.

The sun has become a niche for the light of His Power. The surface of the sea is a mirror to the light of that niche and the eyes of dewdrops are all tiny mirrors.

The sun, reflected by the broad surface of the sea, is also reflected by the drops on the wrinkles on its forehead. The tiny eye of the dewdrop also shines with it, like a star; they hold the same identity.

From the perspective of the sun, the dewdrop and the sea are the same; its power makes them equal. The pupil of the dewdrop's eye is a tiny sun.

The magnificent sun also is a tiny dewdrop; the pupil of its eye is a light received from the Sun of Power and it is the moon to that Power.

The heavens are an ocean; at a Breath of the All-Merciful, drops undulate in the wrinkles of its forehead, which are the stars and the suns.

The Power manifested Itself and scattered gleams on these drops. Every sun is a drop, every star a dewdrop;

Every gleam is a representation – that drop-like sun is a tiny reflection from this manifestation. It makes its polished glass a bulb for that gleam of manifestation, shinning like a pearl.

That dewdrop-like star has a place in its delicate eye for the gleam and the gleam becomes a lamp, with the filament as the eye – and its lamp is lit up.

Multiplicity manifests unity on either side of it

It is a manifestation of Divine Unity that the beginning and end of multiplicity are united at the same point, displaying the Divine Unity.

It is a manifestation of the Divine Power that the changeable power in the universe transforms unity into multiplicity;

Divine Power is distributed among particles and changes in nature, and it is from this that degrees or rays of gravity arise.

These rays are combined – the Maker makes them into a general gravity, which means multiplicity becomes unity.

If you have any merits or qualities, let them remain under the dust of concealment, so they may flourish

O one of renowned qualities! Do not be oppressive by exhibiting yourself; if you remain under the veil of concealment, you will be a source of favors and blessings for your brothers;

Also, you brothers will benefit from or have a share in your merits; it is even possible that every brother of yours will become like you – this will attract respect to each of them.

But if you emerge from concealment and exhibit yourself, although respected and magnanimous under it, you will become an oppressor in the open. There you were a sun, here you will overshadow others.

You will cause your brothers to lose respect. That means, self-manifestation and being distinguished individually are despotic attitudes.

If this is true of the manifestation of genuine qualities, what place remains for acquiring fame through lying artifice and hypocrisy? This is a profound mystery, and it is in accordance with this that the Divine Wisdom and the perfect order It has established

Draw the veil of concealment over an exceptional individual within their species, thus enhancing the value of the entire species and making it appreciable.

Examples for you: saints among humankind and the appointed hour within a lifetime are unknown, indefinite. Concealed within Friday is an hour when prayers are accepted.

Hidden in the month of Ramadan is the Night of Power and Destiny. Concealed among the All-Beautiful Names is the elixir of the Greatest Name.

It is their being undefined that creates the splendor in these examples – the splendor of the whole of humanity thanks to the saints among it, the whole day of Friday due to the hour when prayers are accepted, and the entire month of Ramadan due to the Night of Power and Destiny.

This beautiful mystery also is made manifest through being undefined and is established through concealment. For example:

There is a balance in the fact that the appointed hour being undefined: in whatever state you are, it always maintains the balance between the two pans of fear and hope, working for the next world and for this. And the imagined permanent existence imparts a pleasure to life.

For a life of twenty years with an unknown end is preferable to one of a thousand years with a known end. For after half of it which has passed, with every passing hour you are taking a new step towards the gallows.

Your suffering increases proportionately; there would be no imagined permanence which would afford you solace and you would find no peace.

It is mistaken to feel mercy or wrath greater than God's

One should not feel or show greater mercy than God's, nor should one feel wrath greater than that of God.

So leave matters to the All-Just, the All-Compassionate One, for excessive compassion causes pain and excessive wrath is wrongful and blameworthy.

Worldly recompense proves punishment in the Hereafter

Everyone has experienced this at least once in their lifetime and concludes: "That person has done that evil and has met with what they deserve." This is a principle in life.

This meaningful sentence is frequently expressed by people. The common point in evils of great variety is the very nature of evil.

This means, that an evil, by virtue of its very nature, is subjected to and requires punishment. Minor evils are punished here, while major ones are referred to the Hereafter.

The worldly recompense for evils is a proof of punishment in the Hereafter.

The ease of humankind is inversely proportionate to one's will and power; provision is a broad, gradually-assembled body

O humankind addicted to evildoing! Your free will and power have become the source and reason of your deprivation and troubles. Provision comes in proportion to weakness and impotence.

Once I saw an animal, which was pathetic, skin-and-bones. An able mother had given birth to it together with several others.

While itself could hardly find a morsel to eat, pleasant, nutritious sustenance flowed forth from its mother's teats; the Divine Power provided that sustenance.

That animate being was extremely weak and impotent while motionless in its mother's womb, but there too it received the best, perfect sustenance.

It came to the world while still weak and impotent, and its sustenance was good and relatively perfect.

It grew a little and began to feel it had a certain degree of will-power. It also began confronting troubles and difficulties, therefore parental compassion was still provided to help it.

But when it found itself to have some power along with will-power, it was set free and left to its own devices. Whatever it attempted to do of its own volition caused nothing but confusion.

When it had been unaware of volition, the mechanism of its body, accustomed to working with perfect regularity, caused no confusion, either in its home or in its town.

But when its will-power began to intervene, the order in its life was destroyed and its will-power left it defective. Therefore, we should always say:

"Our Lord! Do not leave us to our own devices in provision during our adulthood!"

And power should always say: "O my Lord! I have put my trust in You both at the beginning and end of everything in my life!"

In the sight of the Divine Power, the provision of an animate being has the same value as its life.

Just as the Power finds an "excuse" and gives that being its life, It also creates its provision and pours it out.

It is as if the Power works with a constant, intense effort, changing and transforming the world of death into that of life, and the dense into the transparent.

Just as It scatters the gleams of life, even into the lowliest of substances, It also sows and stores up providence in everything.

The dead atoms are set to move to meet with the light of life. Some form real bodies, while others form figurative ones.

Provision comes and is united with them. Provision is scattered wide and it is a broad body. In short, life has two bodies,

One is produced and composed, the other scattered. Provision and life are twins, having the same value in the sight of the Power.

It is the Power Which brings forth everything out of non-existence; Destiny arranges the first body in which it is clothed.

The Divine Favoring collects the provisions, the scattered body, and sends this creature to the existent being to be fed.

There is a difference between these two bodies: since life, the first body of the existing being, is a composition, it is visible in its totality.

Whereas provision is scattered and comes in a gradual process, so humankind worries about it. Unless the wrongful will-power of humankind intervenes, the rule is certainly true:

"There is no dying of hunger; a lack of provision does not cause death." There are many reserves deposited in the body, each of which is full.

Many things are deposited in the form of fat. But before this fat is used up, death comes. Therefore, the reason for death is not a lack of provision.

This sustenance is sufficient for a hundred days, but death can come in ten days.

Perhaps a disease arising from altering or abandoning routine nourishment came and caused death while there was still provision.

The lawful provision of carnivorous animals

There is an order and wisdom prevalent in everything; there is no room for chance, even though it appears to be thus due to our inability to comprehend this universal order which has been established by the Divine Wisdom.

Divine Wisdom has assigned as sustenance the numberless carcasses of wild animals for the flesh-eating ones in the animal kingdom.

It has invited these animals to eat these carcasses, so that they can both clean the surface of the earth and find their lawful provision.

So it is unlawful for them to kill a living one to eat in their way of their life. From elephants to vermin and insects,

Millions of beasts die every day, but none of their carcasses appear in the open. This is worth attention; consider the wisdom and the order of

How the originating Power and the profound Wisdom have made animals and humans needy of provision. They have put the halter of need and hunger on them.

They have put living beings in order through this halter, making them travel within the sphere of need, without allowing them to leave the order.

They both preserve the world from going into utter confusion and chaos and make need a springboard for progress in human life.

Wastefulness leads to dissipation, dissipation leads to poverty

My wasteful brother! Two morsels have the same amount and quality of nutrition, but one costs one *kurush* (cent), the other, ten;

They are also equal both before they enter the mouth and after they have passed down the throat. Only for a few seconds in the mouth do they give delight to the "intoxicated" sense of taste.

The only difference lies in their tastes, which is a cause of deception; the sense of taste is in fact a doorkeeper and inspector for the stomach.

But the deception causes its misuse. By only tipping the doorkeeper and gratifying it – giving a passing delight to the sense of taste,

One can confuse it in the fulfillment of its duty. Spending eleven *kurush* instead of one is a satanic habit.

It is one of the worst ways, one of the worst types of wastefulness: do not seek it.

The sense of taste is an informer; do not seduce it with pleasures

The Divine Lordship's Wisdom and Favoring have made, with the mouth and nose, two centers within you, which form a frontier post. They also have appointed correspondents.

In this microcosm – man, God has made the blood-vessels telephones and the nerves telegraphs, appointing the telephones as assistants to the sense of smell (nose) and the telegraphs to the sense of taste (mouth or tongue).

Out of His Mercy, that True Provider has embedded instructions in all kinds of food: flavor, color, and smell.

Thus, these three attributes are proclamations, invitations, permits, and heralds from the All-Providing: those who are needy and desire food are attracted through them.

He has given the senses of taste, sight, and smell to the animals needy of provision as tools. He has also adorned food with various decorations.

He soothes desirous souls, and attracts the indifferent and idle by exciting them.

When the food enters the mouth, the sense of taste immediately sends telegraphs to every part of the body. The sense of smell telephones, informing us about the type of the food.

The senses and organs that are needy of provision act each according to their need and make the necessary preparations – they either admit or refuse.

Since the sense of taste is a telegrapher, charged with sending telegraphs by Divine Favoring, do not seduce it with pleasures.

For then it will forget what true appetite is; false appetite emerges and pesters it, bringing illnesses and addictions as penalties.

True pleasure springs from true appetite, true appetite from true need; this essential pleasure is sufficient for king and beggar alike, and makes both equal.

Also, while a *dirham* (cent) suffices for that pleasure and soothes the pain of both need and appetite, spending a *dinar* (dollar) is wastefulness and its value is reduced to that of a *dirham*.

Like intention, point of view may transform habitual actions into worship

Note this point! Just as through the intention (to lead a life that is pleasing to God), permissible habitual actions may become worship, so too according to the correct point of view, the physical sciences may become knowledge of God.

If you study and reflect, that is, if you look at things as signifying one other – their Maker – and in respect of the art they contain, you will utter: "How beautifully the Maker has made this, how well He has done it!" instead of "How beautiful it is."

If you look from this point of view at the universe, the gleams of purposes for its existence and of its perfection shining from the designing of the Eternal Designer, and the order and wisdom will illuminate your doubts;

And the sciences of the universe will become knowledge of God. But if you look at things as signifying themselves from the point of view of "nature," and from the point of view of "How have they come into being by themselves?" –

If you look thus at the universe, all of your scientific knowledge will be only ignorance. Ownerless truths become thus worthless in worthless hands. The testimonies to this are many.

Merely naming something is sometimes a reason to substitute full knowledge of it

Here is a light, but it darkens or is illuminated darkness – in the present way of thinking, it transforms simple ignorance into compound ignorance.

They give a glittering name to something that is unknown and think that by so doing they have attained full knowledge of it.

Comparing this to other unknown things, they suppose that they have explained them, whereas defining and explaining something means having a full picture of it.

Giving a mere name – the one who gives it is ignorant, and although it appears to the eye to be bright and attractive, its aspect that is connected to the thing named is dark:

It is possible neither to define nor explain with it; only the mind is deluded. Examples of this are many, such as:

General gravity, magnetic force, electric power, telepathy, vibration, and magnetism…

At this time, the Shari'a does not permit affluence

When pleasures call us, we should say: "*Sanki Yedim* (It is as if I have eaten it.)" For someone who made this a rule did not consume a mosque!

Formerly, most Muslims were not hungry, so ease and comfort were permissible to a certain extent.

Now, however, most have fallen hungry, and the Shari'a no longer permits a pleasurable life.

The livelihood of the mass of Muslims, of the majority of the innocents, is simple. So following them in their simple life is a thousand times preferable

To being like the extravagant minority, or the few profligates, in their luxurious lives.

Your pleasure lies in your pain and your pain in your pleasure

O one stricken by calamity!

Pains should urge you to this: You should welcome and smile at temporary pains rather than temporary pleasures.

Pains resemble bees: if you disturb them, they crowd around you, but if you remain indifferent to them, they scatter around to their work.

Whoever "turns back" to think of their past life, their heart or tongue will utter either a sigh of grief or a sigh of relief or words of praise and gratitude for God.

It is a hidden pain in the spirit that is translated by a sigh of grief, while the sigh of relief or the utterance of praise and gratitude for God informs us of a bounty and pleasure in the heart.

The memory of pleasures that remained in the past cause both the heart and the tongue to utter sighs of grief.

For, in the same way that the cessation of pain is pleasure, the cessation of pleasure is pain. Even thinking of or remembering the cessation of pleasure gives the spirit unceasing pain.

It is because of this that each of figurative loves – love for the opposite sex – is a collection of laments, arising from the pain caused by the fear of their cessation.

But the cessation of past pains leads both the heart and the tongue to utter sighs of relief and words of gratitude for God.

The disappearance of a day's pleasure is a perpetual pain, while the disappearance of a day's pain is a perpetual pleasure in the spirit.

The human conscience or consciousness always desires unending pleasure and bounty. This lies in love and knowledge of God, reflection, and spiritual perfection;

It also lies in spiritual gifts that pour into the heart, in gleams of the truth, and in the pursuit of true happiness. These are all possible through, and are based on, belief and certainty of belief in and knowledge of God.

Sometimes the absence of bounty is a bounty

Memory is a bounty, but forgetfulness is preferable for an amoral, heedless person at times of calamity.

Forgetfulness is also a bounty; it allows one to suffer the pains of only the present day but makes one forget accumulated sorrows.

There is a bounty in every calamity

O calamity-stricken one! Within the calamity is a bounty. Look closely and you will see it!

Just as in everything there is a degree of heat, so too in every calamity there is a degree of bounty. Consider a worse calamity and then see the extent of the bounty in the lesser one,

And offer abundant thanks to God. For if you are scared by exaggerating it, and you inflate it with complaints, it will grow.

And as it grows it will worsen. If you worry about it, it will double. Its image in your heart will turn into fact.

Calamity will learn from reality, then turn on you and start striking at your heart...

Do not appear important, or you will be degraded

O you with an inflated ego and conceited head! You should understand and consider this criterion: in human society, in the social structure of the human community, everyone has a window, known as status, through which to see and be seen.

If the window is higher than a person's height (stature or worth), they will, through pride, try to appear as tall (or taller). But if the window is lower than their height (their stature or the extent of their endeavors for God's sake and for people), they will bend and bow down out of modesty.

In the mature and perfected person, the measure of greatness is to know oneself as low-ranking. While in the defective person, the measure of low-ranking is to feign greatness.

If qualities change places, their natures change

One quality – in different places is sometimes a demon, sometimes an angel, sometimes virtuous, sometimes wicked – some examples are as follows:

If an attribute which is regarded as dignity or self-respect for the weak before the strong or powerful is found in the latter, it is pride and arrogance.

If an attribute that is regarded as modesty for the strong or powerful before the weak is found in the weak, it is self-abasement and hypocrisy.

In his office, the gravity of a person of authority is dignity, and his feeling of self-nothingness is self-abasement. But in his house, his feeling of self-nothingness is modesty and his gravity, arrogance.

Forbearance or tolerance on one's own account is good and public-spiritedness, and sacrifice (of one's own right) is also a good deed, a praise-worthy quality.

However, when done on behalf of others, one's tolerance is treachery, and one's sacrifice is a wicked attribute or act.

Entrusting the accomplishment of an affair to God before taking all the necessary measures and making all necessary arrangements is laziness, while leaving the desired outcome's realization to Him after doing all that should and can be done is reliance on Him as taught to us by the Shari'a.

Contentment with one's lot or with the results after having exerted one's efforts is praiseworthy contentment, and encourages further effort, reinvigorating one's energy.

But contentment with what one already has is not desirable content-ment; rather, it is lack of the necessary endeavor. There are numerous other examples.

The Qur'an generally mentions good works and piety and righteous-ness without defining them. By leaving them undefined, it alludes to the defining importance of circumstances; its conciseness is in fact a detailed explanation and its silence, an expansive word.

"The truth prevails" is true both in itself and in respect of the consequences

Friend! A questioner once asked: "As 'The truth prevails' is the truth, why are the unbelievers triumphant over Muslims and force or might is triumphant over right?"

I replied: Consider these four points and your difficulty will be resolved. The first point is this. Every means to every truth and right may not be true and rightful at all times.

Similarly, not every means of every falsehood has to be false. The result is a means which (falsehood employs and) is true prevailing over a false means (which truth or right uses). In which case, a truth is overcome by falsehood. But this has occurred temporarily and indirectly, not essentially or permanently.

However, the final triumph is always that of the truth. (It should also not be forgotten that) force possesses a truth, and there is a purpose and meaning in its creation. The second point is this:

While it is obligatory that all attributes of all Muslims are Muslim, in reality this may not always be so.

Similarly, not all the attributes of all unbelievers have to be connected to unbelieving or arise from their unbelief.

In the same way, all the attributes of all sinful transgressors may not be sinful, nor do they need always arise from sinfulness.

This means that an unbeliever's Muslim attribute prevails over a Muslim's irreligious attribute. Indirectly and due to the means, the unbeliever can prevail over the believer.

Furthermore, in this world the right of life is all-embracing. Life – that meaningful manifestation of the universal Mercy – has an instance of wisdom, which unbelief cannot impede.

The third point is this: two of the All-Majestic One's Attributes of perfection give rise to two sets of laws. One is the Shari'a of life or of the creation and operation of the universe, which proceeds from the Attribute of Will;

And the other, the well-known Shari'a, which proceeds from the Attribute of Speech.

Just as the commands or laws of the well-known Shari'a are obeyed or disobeyed, so too do people obey or disobey the Shari'a of life.

The reward and punishment for the former is received mostly in the Hereafter, while the penalties and rewards of the latter are suffered mostly in this world.

For example, the reward of patience is success, while the penalty for laziness is privation; and the reward of labor is wealth.

The reward of steadfastness is triumph. The punishment of poison is illness and the reward of its antidote is health.

Sometimes the commands of both Shari'as are in force in a single thing; it has aspects pertaining to each.

That means, obedience to the rules of life is a truth, and obedience prevails, while disobedience to it is a false attitude.

If a truth has been the means to a falsehood, when it prevails it will be the true means to a falsehood. This is an example of truth being defeated by a falsehood owing to the means. It is not the defeat of the truth itself by falsehood.

In consequence, "The truth prevails" means: "The truth is triumphant essentially or in itself." Also, the end or consequence is intended.

The fourth point is this: a truth has remained in potential or it is powerless, or adulterated or contaminated. It needs to be developed or given fresh strength.

In order to improve and brighten it, falsehood is temporarily allowed to attack it, so that however much pure gold of truth is needed will emerge unadulterated.

Even if in the beginning falsehood is victorious in this world, it cannot win the war. *"The final (happy) outcome is in favor of the God-revering, pious,"* will strike it a blow!

So falsehood is defeated. The truth of "The truth prevails" inflicts punishment on it. See: the truth is triumphant.

Some social principles

If you want some principles for social life: justice which is not egalitarian is not justice.

The same age and status or social standing cause rivalry and conflict. Being complementary and congruous is the basis of solidarity.

An inferiority complex provokes arrogance. A weak character is the source of haughtiness. Impotence gives rise to opposition.

Curiosity is the teacher of knowledge. Need is the master and wheel of progress. Boredom and distress are the teachers of dissipation.

Thus, the source of dissipation is distress and boredom. As for distress, its mine is despair, pessimism, and evil-suspicion, as well as misguidance in thought, darkness in the heart, and misuse of the body.

Low civilization has destroyed respect toward women

> When foolish men become womanish by following their fancies,
> Rebellious women become masculine through impudence.

Low civilization has turned women into common goods and destroyed respect toward them.

The Shari'a of Islam mercifully says that it is (basically) their homes where women will enjoy true respect; in their homes, in family life, they are comfortable.

Cleanliness is their adornment, their magnificence lies in their good character, their gracious beauty is in their chastity, their true perfection lies in their compassion, and their children are their relaxation and entertainment.

In the face of so many means of corruption, one has to be as strong and unyielding as steel to remain uncorrupted.

If a beautiful woman enters a gathering of "brothers," ostentation and rivalry and envy and selfishness are aroused. Sleeping fancies and passions suddenly awaken.

Uncontrolled freedom for women has caused a sudden awakening and increase of vices in humankind.

Those small dead bodies called pictures, those smiling corpses, have an important and terrible role in the spirit of modern man becoming cross and ill-tempered.[32]

---

32 Just as looking at the dead body of a woman with lust signifies an unparalleled vileness, so too looking desirously at the beautiful picture of a woman who is needy of compassion, which makes her similar to a corpse, extinguishes lofty feelings of spirit.

The prohibited statue is either petrified tyranny, or embodied hypocrisy, or solidified passion. Or it is a talisman that attracts these wicked spirits.

Tendency toward expansion which does not exist in the pious is a tendency to corruption and destruction

O you who are seeking *ijtihad* (new legislation) in Islam to broaden its limits! Consider your body: if the tendency toward its expansion comes from within, it leads to its expansion; but if it comes from without, then it tears your skin.

Similarly, a person sincerely confirms and completely complies with the essential and basic injunctions of Islam: the tendency toward expansion in such a person is a tendency toward perfection.

However, the same tendency in another who is outside the sphere of obedience to Islamic essentials and indifferent to them is a tendency toward corruption and destruction.

At this time, repeatedly afflicted by "storms" and "quakes," it is necessary not to open the door to new legislations, but rather to shut even the windows.

Those heedless and indifferent in belief and the practice of the Religion should not be indulged with dispensations; they should rather be warned strictly and aroused with heavier responsibilities and greater care.

The scope of Divine Power rejects intermediaries and helpers

For the All-Powerful One of Majesty, in relation to the scope of the control and operations of His Power, our sun is like a particle.

In order to have some glimpse of the vastness of the control and operations of His Power in a single realm of beings, take the gravity between two atoms, and then go and put it beside the gravity between the sun of suns and the Milky Way.

Bring an angel whose load is a snowflake to a sun-like angel who holds the sun; put a needle-fish beside a whale;

Then consider all at once the vast manifestation of the Eternal All-Powerful One of Majesty and the infinitely perfect "workmanship" in things, from the smallest to the greatest.

The things in circulation such as gravity, conductivity, permeability or pervasiveness, and laws – these are only names for the manifestations of His Power and the instances of His Wisdom;

They can and indeed have no other meaning or function. Think of them together and you will necessarily understand that claiming the existence of efficient or creative causes and means and attributing to Him helpers and partners is all false,

All is illusory and deluding in the face of that Power. Life is the perfection of existence; its rank is great and important. Therefore, I say: why should the earth, our world, not be an obedient, subservient entity, like a docile animal?

The Eternal Sovereign has numerous flying animals of this sort in the arena of space, and they are splendid and beautiful.

He has dispersed them through the garden of creation, and set them in continuous motion. The songs of those in space and the activities of these in the world are all words of glorification, acts of worship of the One Who has no beginning and end, the Eternal All-Wise.

Our earth resembles an animate being that displays signs of life. If, to suppose the impossible, it were reduced to the size of an egg,

It would most probably become a tiny micro-organism. If a micro-organism were enlarged to the size of the earth, most probably it would be just like the earth.

If the universe was reduced to the size of a human being, with its stars forming particles, it is possible it would become a conscious animal; reason does not deny this.

This means, the world with all its parts is a glorifying servant of the Ever-Living Creator, the Eternal All-Powerful One, obedient and subservient.

It is not necessary that a thing should be great in size in order to be great qualitatively, for a clock the size of a mustard-seed is more eloquent than a clock the size of Ayasofya (Hagia Sophia).

The creation of the fly is no less, indeed perhaps more, amazing than that of an imposing creature like the elephant.

If a Qur'an were to be written by the Pen of Power in atoms of ether on an atom from this world, in respect of the art it would contain, inversely proportional to its size,

It would be equal to a Qur'an written in the stars on the face of the heavens. The Eternal Inscriber's art is of the utmost beauty and perfection everywhere.

Everywhere it is thus. Everything being of the same degree of perfection proclaims the unity of the Pen and therefore the Divine Unity. Study carefully this most meaningful piece!

The angels are a community charged with the Shari'a of the creation and the operation of the universe

There are two Divine Shari'as (sets of laws), proceeding from two Divine Attributes; two kinds of humans are addressed, one being responsible for each:

The Shari'a of the creation and operation of the universe, which proceeds from the Attribute of Will, orders the circumstances and movements of the universe, the *macro-human*, which are not voluntary. It is the eternally determined system of the Lord, and it is what is wrongly termed "nature."

The Shari'a which proceeds from the attribute of Speech is the set of laws which orders the actions of humanity, the *microcosm*, which are voluntary.

The two Shari'as sometimes are in force in the same kind of beings – God's angels. They are a mighty community, a host of the All-Glorified One.

They are obedient servants and workers, who are responsible for the fulfillment of the first Shari'a; they are representatives, (representing the worship of the inanimate, plant, and animal kingdoms in the Court of God).

Some of them are worshipping servants of God, others are absorbed in knowledge and love of God, stationed near to Him around His Supreme Throne.

As matter is refined, life is intensified

Life is fundamental, basic; matter is dependent on and subordinate to it, and subsists through it. If you compare a microscopic organism with its five senses, and the human senses,

You will see that however much larger a human being is than the microscopic organism, his senses are inferior to the same degree.

The organism hears its brother's voice, sees its food. If it were enlarged to the size of a human being, its senses would be amazing, its life dazzling, and the sight of it like lightning flashing in the sky.

A person is not a living being composed of a dead mass, but a living human cell is composed of billions of living cells.

A human is like the large letters of *Ya Sin*, in which is inscribed *Suratu Ya-Sin*. So *Blessed and Supreme is God, the Creator Who creates in the best and most appropriate form!*

Materialism is a spiritual plague

Materialism is a spiritual plague. It has infected humanity with this terrible fever[33] – it has made it subject to Divine Wrath and punishment. Through insistent inculcation and imitation,

And in proportion to the growth of humankind's ability to criticize, this plague has become severer and spreads ever wider.

It is inculcated by science and imitated in the name of civilization.

Freedom has led to criticism, and misguidance has sprung from the pride civilization causes.

There is nothing idle in existence; an idle person works on account of non-existence

The most miserable, wretched, and distressed person is the one who is idle. For idleness is non-existence within existence, death within life.

Whereas exertion or working hard is the life of the body and the waking state of life!

Usury and interest are absolutely harmful to Islam

Usury causes idleness and extinguishes enthusiasm for work.

The profit of banks, which are the doors of usury and its containers, is always for the worst of humankind, the infidels.

Its profit for the infidels goes to the worst among them, that is, the oppressors.

---

[33] Here the author is referring to World War I.

The profit of the oppressors always goes to the worst among them; that is, the dissolute; it is absolutely harmful to the world of Islam.

The Shari'a does not require nor does it take responsibility for the continual prosperity of all humankind at all costs. For an infidel at war with Islam and Muslims does not deserve respect or legal protection.

The Qur'an defends itself and perpetuates its authority

I saw a man who was stricken by despair and sick with pessimism. He said: "The scholars have decreased in number, and this decrease in quantity causes a decrease in quality. I fear our Religion will die out one day."

I replied: So long as the universe is not extinguished, Islamic belief will not die out.

Also, so long as the public signs of Islam, the minarets of the Religion, the places of Divine worship, the teachings of the Shari'a – all like stakes firmly placed in the earth – so long as they are not extinguished, Islam will always shine.

The mosques are instructors, teaching those who frequent them through their very existence and nature. The public signs of Islam have all become teachers: through the tongue of their very existence and nature, they never fail or forget to inspire the believers.

All the signs are learned teachers, continually teaching the spirit of Islam to those who look on them, causing the world to last through the centuries.

The lights of Islam are as though embodied in its public signs; and the pure water of Islam is as if solidified in its places of worship, each of which is an embodied pillar of belief.

The injunctions of Islam are as though embodied within the public signs; the pillars of Islam are settled solidly in its domains – each is a diamond pillar, and through them the earth and sky are bound together.

In particular, the Qur'an of miraculous exposition is an orator; it has continually been delivering a pre-eternal discourse – no village, no place at all has remained within the Muslim lands

Which has not listened to its address, nor not heard its teaching. According to the meaning of *It is indeed We Who are its guardians and preservers* (15:9), to be a *memorizer* of the Qur'an is a very high station. To recite it is worship for humankind and jinn.

Its continual recitation both teaches and repeatedly reminds of the explicit, incontestable essentials of Islam; it also causes the theoretical matters to become so explicit that they require no further explanation.

These essentials of the Religion have ceased being theoretical matters and have become explicit, easily understood realities. To mention them is sufficient; to remind of them is enough. The Qur'an is constantly a healer (healing the wounds in the minds, hearts, and spirits).

Also, through the constant mentioning and reminding of Islam's essentials, and through the Islamic revival and social awareness they generate, the evidence for all these essentials is evidence for each.

Since social life began in Islam, an individual's belief is not restricted to the proofs particular to themselves, nor is their conviction or conscience based on them alone. Rather, such are also based on innumerable proofs that are located in the common heart of the community.

It is worth noting that as time passes it is difficult to abolish even a weak school of thought. So what about Islam, which is based on the two firm foundations – the Revelation and innate human disposition – and which has ruled so effectively for so many centuries!

With its firmly rooted principles, its profound works, it has cohered to half the globe, becoming a natural spirit. How can it be eclipsed, especially when it has just emerged from a temporary eclipse?

Regrettably, certain abusive infidels have engaged in falsehoods to attack the firm foundations of this lofty palace whenever they found the chance.

They try to shake Islam's foundations. But its principles cannot be attacked, or tampered with. Fall silent now, irreligion! That scoundrel is bankrupt. Enough now of this experiment of unbelief and lies!

The Islamic world's advance-post against the world of unbelief was this *Darulfünun*.[34] But due to our indifference and heedlessness, the snake-like enemy was able

To open up a breach behind the front; irreligion attacked and the nation was shaken. This advance-post, this Paradise-like "garden," illuminated by the spirit of Islam,

---

[34]   *Darulfünun* was the name of Istanbul University during the Ottoman period. This name literally means the House of Sciences. (Tr.)

Should be the firmest, and most truly awakened, in respect of Islam, or it cannot be an institution referred to as the House of Sciences. It must not deceive Islam.

The seat of belief is the heart; the mind is where the light of belief is reflected.

The mind is sometimes a warrior (fighting falsehoods), sometimes it is a broom (removing doubts); if the doubts of the mind do not enter the heart, then the faith and the conscience will not be shaken.

If, as some people suppose, belief is in the mind, many baseless possibilities (circulating about in the mind) can become ruthless enemies to the certainty that is based on experience, which is the spirit of belief.

Heart and conscience are the seats of belief. Intuition and inspiration are evidence for belief. There is another sense which is a way to belief.[35] Thought and intellect, or the mind, are the watchmen of belief.

Rather than instruction in theoretical matters, it is necessary to remind people of Islam's explicit, incontestable essentials

The essentials of the Religion, the explicit, incontestable matters of the Shari‘a, are present in people's hearts; people will be made fully conscious of these if they are continually reminded of them.

The desired result is thus obtained. The Arabic language performs this reminder in a more sublime fashion.

Instruction in theoretical matters is not required in the sermon. Moreover, Arabic discourse is an imprint of unity on the united face of Islam.

The Prophetic sayings (hadiths) say to the Qur'an's verses: It is not possible to reach you!

If you compare the Qur'anic verses and the hadiths, you will see clearly that even the most eloquent of humankind, the conveyor of the Revelation, could not attain the level of the Qur'an in eloquence.

---

35   By the sixth sense Said Nursi means the "senses" or points of reliance and seeking for help that are ingrained in the human conscience; he refers to this in many places of the Risale-i Nur. That is, every human feels the existence of points of reliance or support and seeking help, through which they seek a power to rely on and receive help from particularly in the face of calamities and helplessness. The existence of these senses or points shows the existence of an All-Knowing and Powerful One. (Tr.)

The Qur'an does not resemble his sayings. That means that all the words issuing from Muhammad's tongue were not his.[36]

A concise explanation of the Qur'an's miraculousness

Once I had a dream: I was at the foot of Mount Ararat. The mountain suddenly exploded, scattering rocks the size of mountains all over the world and shaking it.

Then suddenly, a man appeared at my side. He told me: "Explain the aspects of the Qur'an's miraculousness known to you, concisely and precisely!"[37]

I thought of the dream's meaning while I was still in the dream and told myself: the explosion here symbolizes a revolution in humankind.

As a result of this, the guidance of the Criterion of truth and falsehood (the Qur'an) will be exalted everywhere, and will rule. And the time will come to explain its miraculousness!

I said to the questioner in reply: The Qur'an's miraculousness originates in seven universal sources or is composed of seven universal elements:

FIRST SOURCE: This is its brilliant manner of exposition that arises from the fluency of its wording, the eloquence of its meanings, the originality of its concepts, the purity of its language, the beauty of its word-order, and the uniqueness of its styles.

All these elements combined, its miraculousness manifests an amazing embroidery of expressions, and an original linguistic art, thus its repetition never wearies or bores.

SECOND (SOURCE OR) ELEMENT: Formed of the unseen principles underlying cosmic events, and the unseen, mysterious Divine truths, and the unseen realities contained in the heavens, and the events that have become unseen behind the veil of the past, and the matters and events that remain unseen behind the veil of the future,

---

[36]   That is, apart from his own sayings (hadiths), Prophet Muhammad was also the conveyor of the Qur'an, revealed by God. (Tr.)

[37]   Volumes of books have been written on the inimitability of the Qur'an. What Said Nursi says here is a very brief summary. To a certain extent this was explained with examples in The Twenty-fifth Word in The Words. (Tr.)

The Qur'an is the tongue of the Unseen; it speaks with the visible, corporeal world, revealing some matters of the Unseen with subtle, profound and symbolic expressions. It addresses humankind. This is another flash of its miraculousness.

THIRD SOURCE: The Qur'an has an extraordinary comprehensiveness in five aspects: in its wording, meanings, commands, and its knowledge, and the balance in its aims.

Its wording: There are many diverse ways of expression and various aspects in its wording, each being agreeable in the sight of eloquence, grammatically correct, and perfectly suitable for legislation.

Its meaning: The miraculousness of the Qu'ran's exposition at once comprehends and contains the ways of all the saints, the illuminations of those versed in knowledge of God, the schools of those following the Sufi way, the ways of theologians, and the paths of the philosophers.

The extent and variety of what the Qur'an refers to, and the expanse of its meanings: if you look through this window, you will see how broad the arena is!

The scope of its commands: The wonderful Shari'a has issued from the Qur'an; its pronouncements at the same time cover the principles necessary for happiness in both worlds, the means to salvation and security, the relations of social life, the methods of education, and responsiveness to circumstantial realities.

The profundity of its knowledge: The Qur'an mentions or alludes to, at different levels, and with signs and indications, both the physical sciences and the Divine sciences; the Qur'an brings together all the paradisal gardens of all types of knowledge within the castles of its *suras*.

In its aims and purposes, the Qur'an has perfect balance and regular sequence, and it fully conforms to and agrees with the principles of the original Divine pattern and system of creation, and it has preserved the balance thereof.

See the magnificent comprehensiveness in the extensiveness of its words, the breadth of its meanings, the scope of its commands, the profundity of its knowledge, and the balance of its aims.

FOURTH (SOURCE OR) ELEMENT: The Qur'an bestows bounteous, luminous gifts and blessings on every age in accordance with its capacity of understanding and literary degree and on all classes of people in accordance with their capacities and abilities.

Its door is open to every era and every class within each. It is as if this Speech of the All-Merciful is freshly revealed at every instant, in every place.

The Qur'an grows younger as time grows older; its allusions and symbols become clearer and more manifest; that Divine Address rends the veil of nature and causes (ascribing creativity to nature and "natural" causes).

The light of Divine Unity in the Qur'an constantly bursts forth from every verse. It raises the veil of the visible, corporeal world from the Unseen. The loftiness of its address invites humans to be attentive.

The Qur'an is the tongue of the Unseen, speaking to the visible, corporeal world. From this source proceeds its extraordinary freshness, its being an all-encompassing ocean of meaning.

The Qur'an includes Divine condescension to human minds so that they may be familiar with it. The fluency of its styles in various forms makes it lovely to humans and jinn.

FIFTH SOURCE: The Qur'an relates all its narrative accounts and the events they contain with their essential points and presents these in an original, meaningful style as though observing the events at first hand.

Through these narrative accounts of the past events, the Qur'an warns humankind. It relates or tells about former peoples and their experiences, future people and what they will experience, the secrets of Hell and the Gardens of Paradise,

And the truths of the Unseen, mysteries of the visible, corporeal world, the Divine mysteries, and the bonds of creation and the universe. Its styles of narration give the impression that the Qur'an relates what it sees.

Neither time nor the facts discovered over time have refuted the truths of the Qur'an, nor does logic ever contradict them. As for the other revealed Books, which are revered by the world,

The Qur'an relates the points on which they agree in a confirmatory manner, and mentions the subjects on which they differ in a corrective style. All this knowledge and these arguments are related or conveyed by someone "unlettered:" this is a wonder of all times!

SIXTH (SOURCE OR) ELEMENT: The Qur'an was the founder of the Religion of Islam and comprises it. If you reflect on time and place, neither was the past capable of producing the like of Islam, nor is the future.

It is a heavenly rope that holds the earth in its annual and daily orbits, rotating it. It rides upon and weighs down the earth, not allowing it to rebel (against its duty).

SEVENTH SOURCE: The six lights pouring forth from these six sources exist one within the other, and it is from these that a beauty arises, and it is from that beauty an intuition, a luminous means of understanding, emanates.

This produces a pleasure that serves the comprehensive pleasure of its miraculousness, but our language is inadequate to describe this, the mind is also insufficient. That celestial star (of the pleasure in its eloquence) is seen, but cannot be held in the hand.

For thirteen centuries the Qur'an's enemies have desired to challenge it, while it has aroused in its friends a desire for imitation. This too is a proof of its miraculousness.

Millions of books have been written in Arabic as a result of these two intense desires, and have entered the library of existence.

If they are compared with the Qur'an, God's Revelation, if they are weighed on a balance, not only the learned scholar, but even the most common people, who only judge by their eyes and ears, will declare: "This one is heavenly; those are human!"

They will also conclude: "It does not resemble them, it is not of the same class. It is either lower than all of them – and this is self-evidently not true – or

"It is superior to all of them." During that long time from its revelation, the meanings of the Qur'an have always remained open to humankind; it has summoned to itself spirits and minds!

Humankind has employed these meanings, and has adopted them, but it still has not been able to oppose the Qur'an with its meanings; humanity will never be able to do this; now the time of testing has passed.

The Qur'an does not resemble other books; it cannot be compared to them. For due to Divine wisdom it was revealed part by part, over more than twenty years, in response to need and in miscellaneous parts.

The Qur'an was revealed on different occasions; to answer different and repeatedly asked questions, and to legislate judgments concerned with numerous and diverse occasions and circumstances. The times of its revelation were all different.

The conditions where the Qur'an was received and communicated were diverse and varied; the groups of those it was addressing were numerous and remote from one another; the targets of its guidance were numerous and of varying levels.

Based on these foundations, the Qur'an explains, teaches, answers, legislates, orders, forbids, advises, reminds, warns, praises, encourages, condemns, and restrains. Yet despite this, the Qur'an is perfect in eloquence, fluency, mutual proportion, and harmony. The sciences of rhetoric, eloquence, and fine arts testify to this.

The Qur'an has a unique characteristic; none of other forms of speech has it. If you listen to a speech, you will see the speaker (or writer) behind it, or you will find them within it: style is the mirror of the person who writes or speaks.

The Qur'an apparently points to the Prophet, its addressee, who is a veil before the Owner of the Speech. The Owner of the Speech is uniquely the Necessarily Existent Being, Whose words or discourses are infinite and innumerable.

He addresses all His uncountable addressees from eternity in the past to the eternity in the future; however, the Speech of the All-Eternal is only heard in embodied, finite speeches.

He could sum up all His discourse in a single manifestation of His Speech, if it had been possible for us to hear all His infinite words all at once,

Or if all His addressees had been a single ear formed of all the particles of the universe – then that universal ear, that universal light of belief, that inspiration in conscience,

Would have seen the representation of the All-Glorified's Speech behind or in infinite speeches or words in all Its majesty and grandeur.

This means that the variation in the styles of the Qur'an is because the Qur'an comprises God Almighty's condescension and manifestations of His Names and Attributes. This is seen by looking with belief behind His speech embodied in the Qur'an.

Every person can say, "In the world, which was built and is heated and lit up as my home, the sun, that eye of the heavens, smiles at me.

"If God had given it consciousness and speech, that delicate, beautiful entity of the heavens would speak to me and a mirror would be the means of communication with it."

The autonomy of mind gives every individual this right, so they can also say, "My Lord speaks to me from behind His speech, the Qur'an; I see an All-Merciful of Light with my belief."

All beings with spirits, even the whole universe, can say this all together, because there is no congestion or blockage when communicating with Him, (as one's benefiting from the sun does not prevent others from benefiting from it). No one can monopolize or restrict it. He is uncontained in time and space.

O dream-questioner! You asked for conciseness, so I have made an indication. If you want a detailed exposition, that is beyond my capability! A fly cannot watch and scan the sky.

For of its forty aspects of miraculousness, only one is the fluency of its word-order; this could not be explained fully in *Isharatu'l-I'jaz*.[38]

This nearly two hundred-page commentary of mine has been insufficient for that. Rather, I want a detailed exposition from you, as your spirit-inspirations are many.

The fanciful, lust-exciting, genius-impressing, earthly hand of Western literature cannot equal the healing, light-scattering, guiding, heavenly, eternal literature of the Qur'an

Anything pleasing to the elevated taste of the mature and perfected does not gratify childish fancies or dissolute natures.

It does not entertain them. For this reason, one who has grown amid and been fed with base, dissolute, carnal and lusty pleasures will not know spiritual pleasure.

Looking within a perspective fashioned by and based on novels, the present literature, which has issued from Europe, will neither see nor experience the elevated subtleties or the majestic virtues of the Qur'an.

---

[38]   *Isharatu'l-I'jaz* is Said Nursi's commentary on the *Fatiha* (the Opening Chapter of the Qur'an) and the initial verses of *Suratu'l-Baqara*. It covers more than two hundred pages. It is a key to understanding and commenting on the Qur'an. (Tr.)

This literature cannot weigh up or measure the Qur'an by its own scales. There are three arenas in which literature revolves; it roams within their bounds:

Either love and sorrow, or heroism and valor, or a depiction of reality. The Europe-based literature does not seek the truth or acclaim right in heroism; rather, it instills a desire for power by applauding the cruelties of oppressors.

As regards sorrow and love, this literature is not aware of true love; it injects into the soul a lust-exciting thrill.

In the matter of the depiction of reality, it does not look on the universe as Divine art; it does not see it as a painting of the All-Merciful.

Rather, this literature approaches the Qur'an from the point of view of "self-existent nature" or naturalism, and depicts it thus; it cannot free itself from this limitation.

For this reason, what such literature inculcates is a false love of nature. It implants in the heart feelings associated with materialism, from which it cannot easily save itself.

Furthermore, that unmannerly literature is only a sedative and narcotic for the distress of the spirit which arises from the misguidance resulting from materialism; it can provide no remedy.

It has found a single remedy, and that is in novels and fiction. Books are animated corpses, movie pictures are moving corpses. The dead cannot give life!

And the theater – it feels no shame at these three sorts of its fiction resembling "reincarnated" ghosts from the vast grave known as the past.

It has put a false, lying tongue in humankind's mouth, attached a lustful eye to its face, clothed the world in a scarlet dress, and does not recognize pure beauty.

If literature indicates the sun, it puts in the reader's mind a beautiful blonde actress; but it apparently says: "Dissipation is bad; it is not fitting for humanity."

Literature indicates harmful consequences. But its depictions so incite dissipation that they make the mouth water and reason cannot maintain control.

They rouse appetite, excite desire, thus the emotions heed neither advice nor warnings. The literature of the Qur'an, however, stirs up no such desires;

It imparts love of and attachment to right, a passion for pure beauty and pleasure in it, and zeal to attain and establish the truth. It never deceives.

The Qur'an does not look at the universe from the point of view of "self-existent nature" or naturalism; it speaks of it as Divine art, as a painting of the All-Merciful. It does not confuse the mind.

It inculcates the light of knowledge of the Maker. It indicates His signs in all things. Both the literature of the Qur'an and that of the modern age can produce a touching pathos, but they do not resemble each other.

The literature born of Europe excites a pathetic sorrow that arises from a lack of friends, from being ownerless; this is not an elevated sorrow.

This literature is a despairing sadness inspired by a deaf nature and blind force. It knows and shows the world as a desolate wasteland, and not in any other way.

The literature depicts the world in this way, and it takes the sorrowful and places them, ownerless, among strangers, leaving them without hope.

Due to this emotional mood the literature has imbued them with, they gradually move to misguidance; thus the way is opened to atheism, from whence it is difficult to return. Perhaps they never will return.

As for Qur'anic literature, it produces a sorrow, but it is the sorrow of love, not of orphans. It arises from separation from friends, not from the lack of them.

Its view of the universe, in place of blind nature, is as conscious, merciful Divine art; it does not speak of "blind and deaf" nature.

Instead of blind force, the Qur'an describes the wise and gracious Divine Power. The universe, therefore, does not take on the form of a desolate wasteland.

Indeed, in the view of those with sacred sorrow to whom it is addressed, the Qur'an becomes a gathering of friends. On every side there is mutual love and responsiveness, which cause no distress.

There is friendliness at every corner, giving the sorrowful in that society a yearning sorrow, an elevated feeling, not a dejected grief.

Both give rise to eagerness. But through the eagerness that is pro-voked by alien literature, the carnal soul becomes excited, fanciful desires are stimulated; there is no joy to the spirit.

The Qur'an's eagerness, however, excites the spirit, spurring one on to lofty aims. It is for this reason that the Shari'a of Muhammad, upon him be peace and blessings, does not desire play nor pastime.

It has forbidden some (musical) instruments for amusement, and per-mitted others. That is to say, instruments that produce Qur'anic sorrow and eagerness are not harmful.

But if such music produces the despairing grief of the orphan or carnal excitement and eagerness, then the instrument is prohibited. It changes from person to person, not everyone is the same.

There are two viewpoints, one dark, the other illuminating

There are two viewpoints, and two kinds of investigation. One is increas-ingly illuminated and brightened, while the other is increasingly drowned in doubts, with the result that the mind is darkened.

For example: There is delightful, sweet water, flowing from a source. It flows in thousands of canals. Foul things may mix with it in some places.

A person sees the source, tastes the water, and understands that it is sweet. They conclude that the foulness is not from the source.

Whenever one passes by a canal or waterway, the smallest sign that the water is pure and sweet convinces them of its original sweetness and purity.

Only an otherwise decisive, substantial proof can contradict such a sign. Then the person says: "Some other substance has become mixed with this pure, sweet water."

This way of investigation strengthens belief, expands and exhilarates the heart, and develops and flourishes the truth. It is this splendid view-point that is encouraged by the Qur'an.

The other viewpoint is faulty and harmful. A foolish one walks with it around the canals unconsciously, instead of beginning from the source.

Their eyes are fixed on the ground; whenever they encounter a canal and see a doubtful sign that the water is bitter,

They doubt that the water is sweet. In order to judge that it is sweet, they seek a conclusive proof.

They desire to base the overwhelming result produced from a huge, pure source on one very insignificant sign.

Their doubt increases (as they encounter some insignificant foulness mixed with the water from the outside), and they begin to lose their former conviction, and become a target of groundless suspicions. The recompense of such a viewpoint is an increase in error.

Their intellect is defective, the principles they follow are flawed, and their capacity for understanding is narrow.

If they cannot reach the truth, they return and say: "This is not the truth," refuting and denying it.

There is a proverb among the Kurds: A bear stood under a vine, and not being able to reach the grapes, said, "Woe to these! They are foul and sour!"

Branches offer fruit in the name of Mercy

Apparently, the branches of the tree of creation extend the fruits of bounties to the hands of living beings on every side.

But in reality it is a Hand of Mercy, a Hand of Power, Which holds out to us these fruits on those branches.

You should kiss that Hand of Mercy in gratitude; you should thankfully proclaim the holiness of that Hand of Power.

An explanation of the three ways indicated at the end of Suratu'l-Fatiha

O brother full of aspirations! Taking your imagination with you, come with me. See, we are in a land, we look around. There is no one to see us.

A layer of black clouds has settled on the high mountains, which are like tent-posts. The clouds have also overshadowed the part of the earth where we are.

They form a solid ceiling over us, but some say its six sides are open and the sun is shining there. However, we are under the cloud and the darkness oppresses us.

The distress is suffocating; the lack of fresh air is killing us. Now three ways are open to us. One is an illuminated realm; I looked upon it once. I also came here once before; I have been to the third realm as well.

The first way extending before us is this: most people take it and it is the way through the world, inviting us to travel it.

See, we are on our way, going on foot. See the boiling sands of this desert, how they are scorching us with their anger, threatening us!

Look at the mountainous waves in that sea; they are furious with us too. Now thank God, we have reached the other side, we can see the sunlight.

But only we know the difficulties we have suffered. Alas! We have returned to this same wasteland, the dark ceiling of cloud hovering over us. What we need is a wonderful light-filled realm,

Which will brighten the eye of the heart; if you have the courage, we will enter this extremely risky way together to reach this destination.

Our second way: we will plunge through "nature," and pass to the other side. Or we will go trembling through a natural tunnel.

I traveled this way once before, full of entreaties and prayers, without feigning reluctance before God. But on that occasion I had with me a substance to smelt and rend "nature."

The Qur'an, the miraculous guide of the third way, gave it to me. Brother, stick close behind me, and have no fear!

See, here await tunnel-like caves and underground torrents. They will let us pass. Let neither nature nor these awesome lifeless beings frighten you in any way!

For behind its sour face the smiling Face of its All-Compassionate Owner – I perceived It through the light of that radium-like substance of the Qur'an.

How happy you are! Now we have come out into the light-filled world; see this graceful earth, this pleasant and lovely heaven.

Raise your head! See, this Touba-tree invites us – it grows high into the heavens, has rent the clouds, leaving them far below.

It is the Qur'an. It has spread its branches everywhere. We must hold onto this branch which is trailing down, so that it can raise us up.

One of the manifestations of that heavenly tree on earth is the Illustrious Shari'a. This means we ascend to this world of light in that way without difficulty; we will not be shaken by distress.

As we have gone wrong, we will now return to our former place and find the right way.

See, *our third way*! Over the mountains hovers a Royal Falcon, reciting the *adhan* to the whole world.

See, the supreme *muadhdhin*, Muhammadu'l-Hashimi, upon him be peace and blessings, is calling humankind to the luminous world of light. He enjoins supplication and obligatory Prayers.

Look at those mountains of guidance! They have rent the clouds and have reached as high as the heavens. See those mountains of the Shari'a, how they have adorned the face and eye of the earth!

Now we must take off from here in lofty aspiration and endeavor. For the light and breeze are up there; the radiant face of grace is there. Ah, now here is the Uhud[39] of Divine Unity, that mighty, beloved mountain.

Here is the Judi[40] of Islam, that mountain of salvation and safety. Here is the Mountain of the Moon[41], which is the bright Qur'an; the "Nile," the pure water of life and mercy, flows from that sublime source. Take a drink of its sweet water!

> So Blessed and Supreme is God, the Creator Who creates in the best and most appropriate form! (33:14)

> And their final call is "All praise and gratitude are for God, the Lord of the worlds!" (10:10)

Friend! Now cast away your imagination and don your reason! The first two ways are those of "*those who have incurred Your wrath*" and "*those who are astray.*"

---

[39]   Mt. Uhud is a mountain in Madina, five kilometers north from the Prophet's Mosque. A fierce battle took place before it between the Muslim army and the Makkan polytheists during the Prophet's time, in 624. Once God's Messenger, upon him be peace and blessings, said: "Uhud – it loves us much and we love it much too." (*al-Bukhari*, "Fadailu'l-Madina" 6; *Muslim*, "Hajj" 462) (Tr.)

[40]   Mt. Judi is the mountain where the Ark of the Prophet Noah settled following the Flood. See, the Qur'an, 11:44. (Tr.)

[41]   The Mountains of the Moon are the mountain ranges in Ethiopia that were once believed to be the source of the White Nile. The writer likens belief, Islamic belief and life, and the Qur'an to certain mountains. (Tr.)

Their perils are numerous. With these is perpetual winter, their whole year is winter. Only one out of a hundred is saved, like Plato[42] and Socrates.[43]

The third way is easy, and direct and straight. Weak and strong are equal. Everyone may take it. The easiest and safest is this: to be either a martyr or a "ghazi."[44]

Now we come to the conclusion: the first two ways are the path and school of scientific materialism and philosophy. As for the guidance of the Qur'an, the third way is its straight path; it will take us to our destination.

> O God! Guide us to the straight path. The path of those whom You
> have favored (with the blessing of guidance), not of those who have
> incurred Your wrath, nor of those who are astray.

All true pain is in misguidance, and all true pleasure in belief: a mighty truth dressed in imagination

Sensible fellow-traveler! O beloved friend! If you want to clearly perceive the differences between the luminous way of the *Straight Path* and the dark path of *those who have incurred God's wrath* and *those who are astray*,

Come, take your fancy and mount your imagination, together we will go into the darkness of non-existence. We will visit that vast grave, that city full of the dead.

An Eternal All-Powerful One took us out of the darkness of non-existence with His hand of Power, mounted us on existence, and sent us to this world, this city without pleasures.

Now we have come to the world of existence, this fearful desert. Our eyes have opened and we have looked in the six directions.

Firstly, we look before us seeking mercy and help, but tribulations and pain attack us like enemies. We take fright at this and retreat.

---

42 Plato (428–348 BC) was one of the most famous classical Greek philosophers. He was a student of Socrates. He was also a mathematician, writer of philosophical dialogues, and founder of the Academy in Athens, the first institution of higher learning in the Western world. According to him, the material world as it seems to us is not the real world, but only a shadow of the real world. (Tr.)

43 Socrates (469–399 BC) was Plato's teacher and is accepted as one of the founders of Western philosophy. He is known through the accounts of his students, especially those of Plato. He has become renowned particularly for his contribution to the field of ethics. (Tr.)

44 "Ghazi" is an Arabic term which means one who has warred in God's cause. (Tr.)

We look to left and right to the natural elements, seeking help. But we see their hearts are hard and merciless. They grind their teeth, looking at us angrily and threateningly. They heed neither plea nor plaint.

Like helpless creatures, we despairingly lift our gazes upwards. Seeking help, we look to the heavenly bodies, but see them to be threatening.

As though each was a bomb; having shot from of their housings they are speeding through space. But somehow they do not touch one another.

If one confused its way accidentally, this visible, corporeal world would be blown to pieces; God forbid! They move dependent on chance; no good can come of them.

In despair we turn back our gaze from that direction, overcome by painful bewilderment. We bow our heads, bent over our breasts; we look to ourselves, pondering and studying our own selves.

Now we hear the shouts of myriad needs coming from our wretched selves. The cries of thousands of desires issue forth. While hoping for solace, we take fright.

No good comes from that either. Seeking refuge, we consult our conscience or conscious nature; we look into it seeking a means and seeking help. Alas, again we are left unaided; we have to help our conscious nature.

For in it are thousands of aspirations, seething desires, wild emotions, all extending throughout the universe. We tremble with all of them, and cannot offer help.

Left unaided between existence and non-existence, these aspirations extend to eternity in the past on one side and eternity in the future on the other. They are so extensive. Even if the conscious nature were to swallow the world, it would still not be satisfied.

Whatever we have had recourse to on this painful path, we have encountered calamities. For the paths of *those who have incurred God's wrath* and *those who are astray* are thus. It is chance and misguidance which lead us on these paths.

It is we who have allowed chance and misguidance to lead us, and so we have fallen into our present state. We are in such a state that we have forgotten the beginning of existence and the end of the world, as well as the Maker and the resurrection of the dead.

We are in a state that is worse than Hell; it scorches more terribly and it crushes our spirits. We had recourse to these six directions, but the result was this state.

It is a merciless state, comprising fear and terror, impotence and trembling, alarm and isolation, being orphaned and despair.

Now we will take up fronts opposite each of the directions (from where we had sought mercy and help, only to fall into a merciless state) and try to repulse them. Firstly, we have recourse to our own strength, but alas! We are powerless, weak.

Secondly, we turn to our souls, hoping their needs can be silenced. But alas! We see that they cry out unceasingly.

Thirdly, we cry out for help, seeking a savior; but there is no one to hear and respond. We think everything is hostile, everything strange. Nothing consoles our hearts; nothing gives a sense of security or true pleasure.

Fourthly, the more we look at the celestial bodies, the more they fill us with fear and awe. A feeling of terrifying loneliness, which vexes the conscience, appears; it torments the mind and fills us with delusions.

Brother! That is the path of misguidance! On it we experienced all the darkness of unbelief. Come, now, my brother, we will turn again to non-existence.

Again we will come. This time our way is the Straight Path and the way of belief. Our guide and leader are Divine Grace and the Qur'an, the Falcon that flies over the centuries.

At one time, the Eternal Sovereign's Mercy and Grace willed our existence, His Power brought us forth, graciously mounting us on the law of His Will, completing us stage after stage.

Then It compassionately clothed us in the garment of existence, bestowing on us the rank of undertaking the Supreme Trust,[45] whose decorations are supplication and the obligatory Prayers.

All of these stages are mansions of bestowal on our long road. To make our journey easy, the Divine Destiny has inscribed a decree on the parchment of our foreheads;

---

[45]   The Supreme Trust is the human ego or being human or human nature as the focus of the manifestations of God's Names that are manifested throughout the universe. (Tr.)

Wherever we go, with whichever group we are guests, we are welcomed in truly brotherly fashion. We give of our belongings, and we receive from theirs: a delightful trade.

They nourish us, adorn us with gifts, then see us off on our way. Now at last we have come to the door of the world. We hear a noise.

See, we have arrived on the earth. We have set foot in the visible world. Here is a promenade and festival, organized by the All-Merciful for the clamorous habitation of humankind.

We know nothing at all, our guide and leader is the Will of the All-Merciful. Our delicate eyes are the deputy of this guide. We open our eyes and look around. Do we recall the former time from where we came?

We were strangers, orphans, we had many enemies. We did not know who our protector was. Now, with the light of belief, which is a strong pillar, we find in us a point of support and a point of help against those enemies.

Our protector, belief in God, repulses our enemies. It is the light of our spirits, the light of our lives, and the spirit of our spirits. Now our hearts are easy and we disregard the enemies, not even recognizing them as such.

When on our former journey we consulted our conscious nature, we heard innumerable cries, laments, and complaints.

And so we were overcome by calamities. Now, our aspirations and desires, our capacity and senses, constantly desire eternity. But we did not know how to obtain it. We were ignorant of how to obtain it and our conscious nature lamented and cried.

However, all praise and gratitude be to God, this time we have found a point of help; it constantly gives life to our capacity and aspirations, making them take flight for eternity.

It shows them the way, and from that encouraging, mysterious point – belief in God – our capacity receives help, drinks the water of life, and races to its perfection.

The second pole of belief is affirmation of the Resurrection, the resurrection of the dead and eternal happiness. Belief is the pearl of this shell and the Qur'an is its proof. Human conscience is a mystery indicating it.

Now raise your head and take a look at the universe. Speak to it. On our former way how awesome it appeared. Now it is smiling on every side, gracefully winking and speaking.

Do you not see – our eyes have become like bees? They fly everywhere in the garden of the universe, around the multitude of flowers; each flower offers these bees delicious nectar.

Each flower also offers friendliness, solace, and love. Our eyes collect them and bring back the pollen of testimony. They make the most delicious honey flow forth.

As our gaze alights on the movements of the heavenly bodies–the stars, or suns–they give the Creator's wisdom in its hands. Learning important lessons and the manifestation of His Mercy, it takes flight.

It is as though the sun is speaking to us, saying: "My brothers and sisters! Do not feel lonely or frightened. You are welcome, how good of you to have come! This dwelling place is yours; I am but a candle-holder.

"I am like you, naught but a pure, absolutely obedient servant. Out of His utter mercy, the Unique and Eternally Besought One has made me a servant of light for you. Light and heat are from me, supplication and Prayer from you!"

Now look at the moon! And the stars and the seas; each says in its own tongue: "Welcome! It's good of you to have come! Do you not recognize us?"

Look through the mystery of cooperation, lend an ear to the signs of the order. Each says: "We are all servants, mirrors of the All-Majestic One's Mercy; do not worry, do not become weary or fearful of us!

"Let not the roars of the thunder and cries of events rouse in you fear or suspicion, for within them reverberate Divine recitations, glorifications, supplications, and entreaties.

"The All-Majestic One, Who sent you to us, holds their reins in His hands. The eye of belief reveals the signs of Mercy on their faces; each proclaims It."

O believer with a wakeful heart! Let our eyes rest a little; now in their place we will hand over our sensitive ears to the blessed hands of belief. We will send them to the world to listen to its delightful tune.

The voices and sounds that we thought were universal mourning and lamentations of death on our former way are in fact supplications and prayers, cries of glorification.

Listen to the murmuring of the air, the twittering of birds, the pattering of the rain, the splashing of the seas, the crashing of thunder, the crackling of stones; all are meaningful sounds of prayer and glorification.

The melodies of the air, the roars of the thunder, the strains of the waves are all recitations of Divine Grandeur. The chanting of the rain, the chirruping of the birds are all glorifications of Mercy – indications of truth is uttered in their languages.

The sounds of things are all sounds of existence: "I too exist," they say. The silent-seeming universe speaks uninterruptedly: "Do not suppose us to be lifeless, O chattering fellow!"

It is either the pleasure of bounty or the descent of mercy that makes the birds sing. With their different voices, their songs, they applaud mercy, alight on bounties, and take flight with thanks.

Implicitly they say: "Beings of the universe, O brothers and sisters! What fine conditions we live in; we are tenderly nourished, we are happy with our lot!" With beaks pointed to the heavens they send their cheerful songs through the air.

The universe is a lofty orchestra in its entirety; its recitations are heard through the light of belief. For wisdom rejects the existence of chance and the order in existence banishes any formation or event from being attributable to random coincidence.

Fellow-traveler! We are now leaving this world of representations, stepping down from the realm of images. We will stop in the field of reason, follow the ways we have traveled that lie before our eyes and compare them.

Our first, painful way is that of *those who have incurred God's wrath*, and *those who are astray*. It inflicts suffering on the conscience, in its innermost part; suffering and severe pain. Consciousness shows this; we traveled that way in opposition to our conscience.

We must be saved from it, we need to be – either the pain must be alleviated, or human feeling numbed – we cannot endure it otherwise, for our cries for help are not heeded.

Guidance is healing, but carnal tendencies and fancies block out the feelings. Submission to carnal tendencies and fancies requires solace, and solace requires forgetfulness, distraction, occupation, and entertainment

So that those elements of deception can fool the conscience and put the spirit to sleep, stopping it from feeling any pain. Otherwise, that grievous suffering scorches the conscience, the lamentation is unendurable and the anguish of despair cannot be borne.

This means, the farther one deviates from the Straight Path, the more one is stricken by this state, and the conscience cries out. Within every pleasure is a pain, which is a trace of this state.

This means that the glitter of civilization, which is a mixture of fancy, lust, amusement and dissipation, is a deceptive cure for the terrible distress that arises from misguidance; the glitter is a poisonous narcotic.

My dear friend! On our second way, that light-filled road, we perceived a state of mind in which life becomes a source of pleasure, and pain joy.

We understood that the second way imbues the spirit with a state that has various degrees according to the strength of belief. The body receives pleasure through the spirit and the spirit receives pleasure through the conscience.

An immediate pleasure is felt in the conscience; a spiritual paradise is present in the heart. Reflective thought opens up that pleasure only to increase it, while consciousness unveils secrets.

The more the heart is aroused, the more the conscience is stimulated and the spirit stirred, the greater the pleasure; fire is transformed into light and winter into summer.

The doors of paradises open up in the conscience and the world becomes a paradise. Within it our spirits take flight, soaring like falcons and kites, entreating, praying.

Dear fellow-traveler! Farewell for now. Let us offer a prayer together and then we will part to meet again!

O God! Guide us to the Straight Path. Amen.

A mystery of the repetitions in the Qur'an

Sometimes fire is seen in light. Repetition to reinforce (a message), reminding to establish (the message), and reiteration to draw attention are all devices that linguists, rhetoricians, and orators make use of.

Just as at every instant human beings are in need of air , of food every day, of light every night, and medicine every year (for every illness), the recurrence of causes (like need) requires the recurrence of effects (like satisfaction),

So too, the intelligence of human beings, which is their most precious means, and their conscience and other deep faculties need the truth at every instant. Every moment, they eagerly desire it and passionately seek Divine manifestations.

They also feel needy of Divine remembrance every hour, and pursue Divine knowledge every day. Since those needs are repeated, the Qur'an guides them to light through repetitions.

The repetitions in the Qur'an are serious reminders and refreshment. Certainly, there are other contexts where repetition could be seen to be a defect; it is only an added decoration for the things that give only pleasure (and not instruction).

For example, repeated consumption of a food gives desirable familiarity with it if it is nourishment essential to the body. Human disposition always seeks the food which it needs and is familiar with.

But if the food is of fruit or sweet, repeated consumption of it leads to boredom and disgust with it.

For any essential, unchanging truth that a word contains, for one that is able to grow – repetition will cause it to be understood more clearly and to become established; this, too, is something the mind wants.

Styles – the form or garment of the word – become worn, so they require variation and renewal, which are agreeable to linguists and rhetoricians.

The Qur'an is thoroughly the food of the heart and the source of power for conscience; it has so great a stature that it reaches the heavens.

It is also the food for spirits and a cure for minds. Its repetitions and reiterations are verification that establishes its truths and enlightenment that reinforces and perfects guidance.

Some of its reiterated truths are the extracts of its food, something that is vitally required for humans. The more they are necessary, the more they are repeated.

While some others are the extracts of the extracts, leaven for truths, and perpetual, embodied lights. The *Basmala* is an example, for which there is, as for air, constant, vital need.

Since the Qur'an is a true and a luminous truth, it is not consumed; rather it gives light and guides to the cure for our "illnesses."

The Qur'anic narrative about Prophet Moses has numerous benefits. The Qur'an has taken the life and Messengership of Prophet Moses in its "bright hand" and employs it for many purposes. The magicians of eloquence cannot help but prostrate before its eloquence.[46]

The experiences of Moses contain great truths and numerous mysteries. They offered excellent, most appropriate examples for the first Muslims, and remain so today;

It is an excellent example for establishing Islam, for understanding the communication of Divine Message, for bearing every trouble and difficulty on God's way, for inculcating certain truths in the hearts of the Muslim Community, and to encourage the people to adopt these truths and the way of implementing them in their lives.

Moses' story also contains the foundations of Divine Messengership and many other basic principles. It is narrated with its different aspects according to the basic theme and purposes of the topic in hand; sometimes to support the messages intended to convey.

In one respect, the narratives about Moses contain the principles of human social life which are so broad and profound that they extend into the depths of both the past and the future. The need to learn the realities of life is as substantial to life as light and food,

Thus, in the same way in which these essential principles and realities of life are repeatedly presented in the Qur'an, so too the lessons that must be learnt are repeated.

Each of the four senses of the spirit has an ultimate purpose

The four elements of conscience are the senses of the spirit: will-power, the mind, the power of perceptiveness or feeling, and the spiritual intellect.

Each of these four senses has an ultimate purpose for its existence: the ultimate purpose for will-power is worshipping the All-Merciful One, while

---

[46] This meaningful piece refers to certain facts concerning Prophet Moses, upon him be peace. One of the miracles bestowed on him was that when he put his right hand under his arm it came forth shining, white. The most skilled magicians of the Egypt of the time prostrated before Moses' miracles of the "shining, bright hand" and that of his staff turning into a serpent. (Tr.)

for the mind it is having knowledge of God. For the power of perceptiveness or feeling, it is love of God, and for the spiritual intellect it is vision of God – a gift of the All-Glorified One.

The perfect form or degree of worship encompasses all these four – it is what the Qur'an calls *taqwa* (piety and righteousness).

The Shari'a both nourishes them, so that they develop, and equips them with the necessary material, directing them to the ultimate purposes of their existence.

There is no creative power in existence save God

Causes are only apparent in creation; if they had actual agency or if they were given creative effect, they should also have been given a universal consciousness. Furthermore, things would have had variable degrees in both structure and art.

However, from the most distinguished to the most ordinary and from the largest to the smallest, eyes have never perceived a fault or incongruity in things.

Everything is perfectly firm and given the utmost care; the Inventor has given to everything a perfect nature according to its stature.

This means that it cannot be said that some things are nearer to the Necessarily-Existent One, while others are farther away.

Due to the perfection and perfect firmness in creation, it can neither be said that the Inventor has needed a means in the invention of some, while in others He has not.

Human beings have been given partial will-power, and it is because of this that there are faults in their actions and works. That is, the lack of firmness in their actions and works shows that they are not compelled to do something by the Creator. Will-power is the base of their accountability for the deeds they commit.

God has made human partial will-power a means for relativity in their arena of disposal; it is required by God's Unity and Wisdom.

It is worth observing that because of human partial will-power a city built by human effort and intelligence is inferior to a beehive – a work of Divine inspiration – in order and arrangement; the former can never be on a par with the latter.

While due to their minimal will-power, the community of bees and the honeycombs – their works of art – are inferior to a pomegranate and a pomegranate blossom – both a city of cells – in order and arrangement.

This means that the Pen Which has inscribed gravity in general is the same Pen from Which particular gravities have dropped into the atoms.

A comparison between the treatment of their saints by Islam and Christianity

The basis of Islam, *There is no creator but He*, rejects the real agency of natural causes and means in the production of things and events.

Islam's basic doctrine of Divine Unity holds that natural causes and means are like letters, which have no significance in themselves. Submission to the Creator guides Muslims to this creed, which the rank of reliance on Him teaches as well. Sincerity in worship also gives it this light.

By contrast, Christianity attributes real agency to causes and means and considers them to have a significant function on their own, like words – that is they have a creative effect; this is misguidance.

The creed of Jesus as the Son of God provides a basis for this creed and for the ways of monasticism and priesthood; the roles ascribed to monks/nuns and priests have guided Christianity to this. This is one reason for its eventual defeat by materialist philosophy.

Christianity views its saints like lamps which have appropriated the light they receive from the sun. This means that saints become the true source of the light that illuminates people.

Viewing humans as a genuine source of light is certain to give rise to the association of partners with God.

However, Islam views its saints as having, like letters, no real or complete function of their own. It knows them to have been enlightened by the light that emanates from the sun and that they only reflect this light, like mirrors.

Not only the saints, but also the Prophets are, according to Islam, mirrors reflecting God's manifestations – that is, they reflect the light that emanates from the Eternal Sun. They are only containers into which the honey of Divine vision is poured; people then take this honey from them.

It is because of this that the followers of the Naqshbandi Sufi Way consider that their guides benefit from the light they reflect.

The guide never knows themselves to be the source of this light; the follower realizes that this guide is a mortal one – and therefore it is impossible for such to be the source of the light.

It is also because of this that initiation into a spiritual way is based on humility or modesty and continues along the path of self-denial until it ends in annihilation before God's Existence.

Only from this point do the stations along the way of the spiritual journeying begin. This destroys arrogance, extinguishes vanity, and kills the carnal, evil-commanding soul.

By contrast, Christianity strengthens the ego with all its faculties and arrogance is not broken. A man with a strong ego, if a Christian, becomes a Crusader;

But if he is a Muslim, his strong ego makes him disregardful of the Religion. This is why unlike Christians the common Muslim people are more religious than the elite.

A significant difference between ecstatic love and knowledge

If saintly, true lovers of God err in following their way or in their interpretations, or in describing Him, their way is, in any event, toward their Beloved. The Beloved One attracts them toward Himself, protecting them from deviance.

For love has an attractive quality, which is fascinated by a heavenly beauty; it is a heavenly attraction. If love is turned toward a true object of love, one who is deserving of true love, then any wrong means will not harm it.

If saints who are distinguished in knowledge of God err in following the way or in their vision or in their speech, they cannot reach their target.

If a way of knowledge is deviant, it will never lead to the intended goal. If the necessary condition is not fulfilled, the result cannot be obtained. Those endowed with knowledge are not like lovers; there are restrictions on their freedom and their free movement.

Those with knowledge of God climb upward by themselves and thus they have to take every step carefully. In contrast, lovers of God are drawn forward and therefore are free of restrictions.

This means, if saintly lovers err, they are in themselves rightly-guided, even though they may cause others to err. But those with knowledge who err mislead both themselves and others. Therefore, they should not be fol-lowed.

It is because of this that certain words of some from among those with knowledge of God – their words implying heresy have led them to mis-guidance and eventually to execution, because such words issuing from them were not open to interpretation and were therefore not tolerated.

But lovers of God – even when some of them have explicitly uttered the same heresy-implying words, not allusively, have continued to be respected by the Muslim Community, which has in no way punished them.

For this reason, even though the heresy-implying words of Muhyid-din[47], Mulla Jami'[48], Ibnu'l-Farid[49] and Ibnu's-Sab'in[50] resembled one another, they were not perceived as being the same and were therefore not treated as the same.

When the knowledge of Muhyiddin, which eventually led him to love, prevailed over his love, his heresy-implying words caused terrible arrows (of criticism) to be shot at him, until Sultan Selim I unveiled the meaning of his words.[51]

---

[47]   Muhyiddin ibnu'l-'Arabi (1165-1240CE): One of the greatest and most famous Sufi mas-ters. His doctrine of the Transcendental Unity of Being, which most have mistaken for monism and pantheism, made him the target of unending polemics. He wrote many books, the most famous of which are Fusus u'l-Hikam and al-Futuhatu'l-Makkiyyah. (Tr.)

[48]   Mawlana Nuruddin 'Abdur-Rahman ibn Ahmad al-Jami' (1414-1492 CE), commonly known as Mulla Jami', is regarded as the last great classical poet of Persia and a saint. He composed numerous lyrics and ballads, as well as many works in prose. His Salaman and Absal is an allegory of profane and sacred love. Some of his other works include Haft Awrang, Tuhfatu'l-Ahrar, Layla wu Majnun, Fatihatu'sh-Shabab, and Lawa'ih. (Tr.)

[49]   'Umar ibn 'Ali ibnu'l-Farid (1181–1235CE) was a Muslim Arab Sufi poet. He was born in Cairo, lived for some time in Makka and died in Cairo. He was esteemed as one of the great-est Sufi poets. Nazmu's-Suluk ("The Poem of Journeying along the Sufi Way") and Hamriyya ("The Ode of Wine"), which is about spiritual bliss, are his two masterpieces. (Tr.)

[50]   Ibnu's-Sab'in was one of saints distinguished with ecstatic love of God. He was born in Murcia, al-Andalus, in 1217 and died in Makka in 1270. He was interested in and wrote on a variety of different subjects and disciplines, such as philosophy, Sufism, science of let-ters (al-'ilmu'l-huruf), literature, alchemy and medicine. (Tr.)

[51]   Muhyiddin ibnu'l-'Arabi once said to those around him in Damascus: "What you worship is under my feet." People were insulted and attempted to kill him, but he escaped. Cen-turies later when Sultan Selim I, the 8th Ottoman Sultan, conquered Syria in 1516, he unveiled the grave of Muhyiddin and ordered excavations to be carried out on the place where he had made the above-mentioned utterance; here some pieces of gold were discov-ered. Said Nursi is referring to this incident. (Tr.)

However, Mulla Jami' was a lover; he uttered the same kind of words explicitly, but he continued to live as a respected man safe from the arrows of criticism.

Ibnu'l-Farid was greater in love and went farther than Muhyiddin in his words, but he received less criticism and was excused.

In the words of Ibnu's-Sab'in, pure love did not appear, so his theoretical words led him to be accused of heresy, and he was not able to save himself from this.

If you say that there are contradictions in Muhyiddin's words, I reply that there may be, but he said whatever he saw. He did not say what he did not see.

However, something should not be expected to be always the same in essence as it is seen to be (in outward appearance). One may judge it differently from how the eyes see it; it can even sometimes be that insight cannot comprehend something in its entirety.

If Muhyiddin said, "I saw!" then it is true that he saw it. He was an exalted spirit, for whom intentional lying was never conceivable; he never lowered himself to telling lies.

The essence of this matter is: he was a traveling spirit, therefore, the unstable, continuously moving manifestations appeared to him as established, unchanging realities. Like seeds, the established, unchanging realities always put forth sprouts.

However, the established, unchanging realities are neither identical to nor different from their moving, unstable manifestations, just as a flower can be neither different from nor identical to its seed. The absolutely accurate balance where every assertion should be weighed is the Qur'an.

If you say, "There are words among Muhyiddin's that they have no place in the Shari'a and because of this some leading scholars considered them to be words of unbelief," I say in reply:

There is an established rule, of which I should remind you. For example, if the Shari'a judges a word or deed to be unbelief and that a believer cannot therefore utter or do it, it means that this word or deed cannot be compatible with belief. It is unbelief, and one who has uttered or done it has committed an act of unbelief, but we cannot therefore judge that person to be an unbeliever.

For they have many other attributes that arise from their belief and which prove that they are a believer. A word or deed uttered or done in certain circumstances or in a different state or mood, and which is open to interpretation, cannot annul their attributes that demonstrate that they are a believer.

We can judge that person to be an unbeliever only when we are certain that that word or deed has arisen from their unbelief; that is, we can only make such a statement when an attribute of unbelief observed in them is the result of unbelief, not of something else.

The heresy- or unbelief-implying words – uttered by persons such as Muhyiddin – are attributable to many reasons and meanings. Therefore, it is doubtful what is meant by them. Because of that, such words cannot be treated as indications of unbelief.

A person's habitual deeds and established attributes that indicate belief prove that they are a believer; suspicion cannot be a basis of judgment.

Doubt cannot always cancel judgment when it is based on certainty. One cannot be accused of unbelief due to a word or deed that can be attributed to forgetfulness or an unintentional error or confusion.

If you say, "In some spiritual ways there are rituals that have taken the form of worship," I say in reply: if they have been adopted with a good intention and meet the following three conditions, they may not be harmful:

They must not be contrary in any way to the decorum and solemnity of Divine remembrance, nor to the manners that must be adopted in God's Presence.

The second condition is that there must never be a religiously forbidden act in them; if there is one, such ways cannot be tolerated.

The third condition is that these acts or actions must not be carried out as part of the worship. They should not be done intentionally either. They should not be anything but that which is done unconsciously and unintentionally out of ecstasy and rapture.

For worship is remembrance itself, while other excusable acts or rituals can be a means of encouragement. The Qur'an has not stipulated any form of remembrance; it has placed no restrictive definitions on a permissible form.

The acts of remembrance may not resemble the acts of worship appointed by the Shari'a. For the acts appointed by the Shari'a are like fruit, both the insides and peel of which are edible.

Whereas the rituals included in Divine remembrance are like walnuts. Their shells are only hard coverings and not edible.

There is a great pleasure in the activities in the universe

Required by the eternal Wisdom, the Hand of Power has included activity in everything so that whatever potential it has may be put into effect;

And It has added an intense pleasure in that activity, making it a significant catalyst or mechanism for the changes in the world.

This mechanism, which is a law, has been made a seed for growth and a wheel for progress. It is the Power Which creates that seed, clothing it in form, and the Mercy nurtures it.

Just as leaving prison to go into an expansive garden is a pleasure, so too, growing into a sprout is an expansive pleasure for the constricted seed.

Transformation starts in the chemical composition and light yields heat. Similarly, when the activity toward transformation begins, pleasure increases and overflows its boundaries.

It is this pleasure which enables the endurance of hardships in the fulfillment of duties and which gives the zeal to carry them out. It is because of this that, when compared to conscious beings, the duties that inanimate beings carry out are faultless.

The activities that inanimate beings are made to do are so attractive that they urge them to work and the inanimate beings thank their Creator by glorifying Him. For they know Him "innately."

It is because of this reality that ease is actually toilsome and the toil that activity entails is ease. An idle one is unhappy, while one who strives is happy; an idle one is rebellious to the order established by the eternal Divine Will, while the one who strives is obedient.

A minority burns in the fire that has been lit to burn the majority.
Otherwise, if responsibility loses its meaning,
the wisdom in testing is lost

An innocent minority suffers from the punishment inflicted on a sinful majority. For human free will requires that the wisdom and mystery of responsibility should remain hidden and open to interpretation.

Religious responsibility is a test which must take place; if the wisdom in testing becomes evident, responsibility no longer involves testing.

Suppose there are two persons in a house which has burnt down; one is innocent, the other sinful and disobedient.

If the innocent one is saved by the Unseen Hand, then not only will human free will lose its meaning, but also responsibility and the wisdom in it.

Responsibility is a means for the development, refinement, and adornment of spirits, which are like raw minerals to be worked.

Through the fulfillment of the orders and through refraining from the forbidden, Abu Bakr, the truthful, loyal one, the renowned companion of the Prophet in the cave, became a diamond, and his purified soul gained refinement and discretion, while Abu Jahl's soul was engulfed in layers of darkness.

Were it not for the wisdom in human responsibility, their souls would not be distinguished from one another, one being a shining star and the other being drowned in darkness; one would not be an illustrious leader while the other was a foul poison.

The wisdom and mystery of responsibility, the difficulties in its fulfillment, the striving and competition in good deeds – these are fire within light.

This fire serves for the purification, refinement, and adornment of souls and the distinguishing of elevated spirits from low ones.

The seed has grown into a tree and the tree has become fruit-bearing.

Weakness is sometimes tyrannical

Despair and suspicion cause a weak spot in the heart. For example: a person so affected sees that the blows of a tyrant hurt the oppressed one.

The blows are terrible; the pains of the oppressed one are reflected in the heart of that weak-hearted one and sadden them.

Sorrows are hurtful and difficult for a weak heart to endure. A person wants to be saved from them, so in order to have ease of heart, they deceive themselves into saying that the oppressed one deserves the blows.

They try to find an excuse and find it: "What business has that lowly one in a place where he will be beaten?"

Thus one becomes wrongful and helps the tyrant. A tiger tears up a weak, miserable creature who cannot escape due to their weakness.

The real cause of this outcome is the ferocity of the tiger, but the weakness of its victim is but an excuse for it. The weak-hearted person lays the crime of ferocity on the weakness of the victim.

The sin of non-existence is condemned to existence.

Greed is the cause of deprivation

Greed brings deprivation, and impetuosity loss. For the Divine law of life has established steps to be taken one after the other in the attainment of the desired goal.

. Since a greedy one does not observe these steps, in most cases they are not able to be successful. Even though they try to observe the steps, greed causes them to leave at least one step untaken; in the end they despair and are engulfed in heedlessness.

However, if Mercy has pity on them, It grants them their desires. Almost everyone has experienced this.

God has created the interior of the heart for belief in and love of Him, as well as for the vision of Him, thus making it delicate.

It is the mirror of the Eternally Besought One; no idol can enter it, for the weight of this "stone" breaks that "glass."

God has made the exterior of the heart also an orderly store for other things. The criminal greed pierces that delicate heart and causes it much trouble.

It imports idols without permission. God is offended by this and punishes the greedy one by making them attain the opposite of their goal.

Those who extend political ambitions and approaches far into the innermost shrine of the Islamic creed meet not with honor and glory, but with disgrace and shame.

They are the objects of disparagement. It is for the same reason that figurative love – love of the opposite sex – usually meets with loss and deprivation.

The collections of poems by those who have fallen in figurative love are full of complaints and wailings and of humiliating lamentations.

For most of the beloveds are tyrannical; they humiliate their lovers and do not pity them.

For figurative love in the interior of the heart is an insult to Divine order and laws of life, it is offensive to them.

The Divine order holds in contempt whatever is contrary to it, and it also disparages such disgraceful and offensive acts and attitudes.

It is because of the principle about greed that two examples from human social life are known to all.

One is greed for sleep; it causes a loss of sleep. The other is that a greedy, importunate beggar does not benefit from charity.

Being over-anxious to sleep and striving to do so in the middle of the night causes one lose it and reach the morning wakeful.

There are two beggars, one greedy and importunate, the other contented, shy, and retiring.

It is to the latter that one wants to give in charity, not the former. Thus does the Divine order urge or punish. There are many other examples like these, demonstrating the universality of this law.

What becomes a Muslim is justice and fairness for God's sake, not egotistical criticism

Our most grievous illness, which is indeed a disaster, is criticism that arises from haughtiness, loquacity, and demagogy. If even a just, truth-loving one engages in such criticism, they injure the truth, while if it is exercised in vanity, it destroys the truth.

What is most grievous is when such criticism is directed against the tenets of the faith and the foundations of the Religion – for faith is both an affirmation and conviction; it is also preference, submission, and observance –

The criticism in question damages submission and observance, preference and compliance. Even though it may not cause doubt, this causes indifference and neutrality in respect of confirmation.

At this time of doubt, suspicion, and ungrounded misgivings, it is necessary for everyone to study and follow sincerely the uncontaminated works that nurture and strengthen compliance and observance, as well as the moving and enthusing ideas and words, free from doubt, that come from illuminated, warm hearts.

What circulates among the tongues of the Western-infatuated fellows is objective or impartial thought and argumentation, whereas this attitude is taking the side of irreligion, even if temporarily.

Only one who intends to enter the Religion or has just entered it can assume this attitude. Or one out of a hundred can assume it temporarily for the purpose of silencing the enemies of the Religion or convincing those who seek the Religion.

However, popularizing it causes the loss of forty Muslims in the hope of winning over one enemy of Islam.

Self-esteem comes from weakness and leads to misguidance: it is deviance among one's comrades, while it is steadfastness against the misleading incitements of hostile unbelievers

One of the sources of misguidance is being proud of one's opinions. One's pride or self-esteem means that their opinions have nothing to do with the "common way of the public" and so they should be taken elsewhere – then one has to build another way for themselves.

One who takes another way than the common way of the public is regarded with doubt and suspicion, and the self-esteemed one feels compelled to fight such doubts and suspicions.

That haughty one, not only is left alone and bereft of the good will of the public, but they also become the object of doubts and suspicions, and people turn against this person. Only one out of a thousand of such people can find salvation.

O one seeking right guidance! Put the head of vanity under your feet and crush it! Enter the formidable castle of belief and follow the way of the believing public.

One sinful and addicted to their lusts does not like the existence of Hell, as it is contrary to the ease of their heart. They welcome anything that, according to their faulty view, contradicts the existence of Hell. With this attitude, a person will go so far as to deny Hell.

The degree of the wickedness of backbiting

Would any of you love to eat the flesh of his dead brother? (49:12)

This noble verse, the Arabic original of which consists of six words, reprimands backbiting with six degrees of severity; it censures backbiting and rebukes it.

The *hamza*, marking the interrogative (and here translated as *would*) at the beginning of the sentence, penetrating like water, reaches into all the words of the verse, so that each of them carries an interrogative accent.

Thus, at the very beginning it asks, "Consider your intelligence: does it permit such an abominable thing?"

It continues to ask: "If you do not have sound intelligence, then look into your heart. If you have a heart, does it love such a grievous thing?

"If you do not have a sound heart, consult your conscience. How can you bite yourself with your own teeth, while it is you who suffers the pain? Also, does your conscience agree with your corrupting social life to such a degree?

"If you do not have social consciousness, then consider your humanity: how can it feel an appetite for such a degree of bestiality that allows tearing fellow human beings into pieces?

"If you have no humanity, consider your human tenderness, your sense of kinship: is it inclined to such a wild act as destroying your own waist?

"Perhaps you have no human tenderness, no sense of kinship; then, at least, do you not have a sound nature, allowing you to tear the respect-worthy dead one into pieces with your teeth?"

This means that backbiting is a chronic disease, which is despised and blameworthy in the sight of the intelligence and heart, the conscience and humanity, human tenderness and a sense of kinship, as well as in both human nature and the Shari'a.

Refuted, rejected backbiting deserves only to be banished. How can one continually drink the blood of humans?

Muslim transgressors are not like the transgressors of other religions; our morality subsists by our Religion

If one among the Muslims is a transgressor, they are usually immoral. Most of them are unfair and unscrupulous. An evil desire can only develop in a Muslim when the voice of belief has been silenced in their conscience.

This means that a Muslim transgressor cannot commit an evil freely without upsetting their conscience and heart, or without demeaning their spiritual values.

It is for this reason that the Religion of Islam recognizes a transgressor as a traitor or criminal; it rejects their testimony. It is for the same reason that Islam judges an apostate as lethal poison.

However, it recognizes the life of a non-Muslim who belongs to a heavenly religion, so long as they follow the public law, or are not at war with it.

What makes a good act good is the good intention behind it. Also, justice must be implemented in the name of the Religion, so that together with the soul, the mind, heart, and conscience can submit to and abide by it.

If a law is promulgated only in the name of the public or political order, it can only rouse fear or apprehension in the heart.

The law can then affect the mind only through apprehension; if one is inclined to a crime they only then consider the formal penalty. They fear the whip of punishment only if it is proven that they are a criminal.

Or they may refrain from a crime fearing that people may reprove them. Equally, they may find comfort in the hope that their crime will remain hidden from people.

It is because of the neglect of the Religion in the execution of justice that justice is no longer respected or effective.

Even though it is implemented in full, justice that is not implemented in the name of the Religion is like a Prayer which is carried out without intention, without facing the direction of the Ka'ba, or without doing the obligatory preparatory ablution – this is Prayer that is not acceptable because some of the obligatory rites are missing.

A believer pays respect to their elders, has compassion for those younger than them, and love and magnanimity for their peers

A ship cannot be sunk because there is a single criminal among its passengers. Similarly, a believer who has many innocent attributes cannot be shown enmity because of a single criminal attribute or act.

In particular, noble attributes, such as belief, confirmation of Divine Unity, and submission to God, which are all means of love, are like Mount Uhud. By contrast, the faults that are means of enmity are like pebbles.

What great foolishness and lunacy it is to consider pebbles as being weightier than Mount Uhud! It is mercilessness of the same degree for a believer to feel enmity toward another believer.

Weighed on the balance of feelings, enmity in believers is contrary to Islam and the security and peace it entails. A Muslim can only feel pity toward their Muslim brother/sister for their faults, and can feel no rancor at all.

In sum: Islam demands brother/sisterhood, and love is essential to belief.

Any person in whom bad moral qualities exist is punished and tormented by these already, while good moral qualities contain their reward in themselves. So refer the case to the All-Just Judge for everyone.

However, the modern scientific approach conceals within it sheer ignorance, for it attributes the works of the All-Powerful Creator to "natural" causes and means and publicizes them as such.

This tremor in humankind, the shaking of Muslim societies, will remove the humiliation caused by the tremor and give them tability. It will probably cause the West to wane and the East to become illuminated.

At one time someone said, "The civilization of unbelievers has brought calamity upon Muslims. Now socialism has appeared, and thrown the world into chaos; its followers are extremely fanatical."

I said in reply: "Never fear! Popular civilization is the goal of socialists. It has principles not so contrary to Islam. Let the West fear it."

But the present, dissipated civilization is peculiar to the elite; it has tried to corrupt Islam and cost it much, bringing about much calamity.

It has taken the greatest "bribe," for it has been kneaded with the leaven of materialism and Inquisition; it is seductive in many respects, equipped with deceptive and inciting elements.

This seditious, enchanting sorcery sells itself to Muslims in return for religion, chastity, and elevated, noble feelings. Offering a glittering life, this deceit corrupts, in multiple ways, both the Religion and chastity.

As for socialism, it offers a simple life and offers itself to the common people. It does not compel people to make sacrifices in return for their religion and chastity; no one feels indebted to it.

Just as people need sustenance, so too they need pleasure. If their need for pleasure is not satisfied with licit, spiritual "food," they seek to satisfy it in evil, lowly, and dissipated ways.

For example, there are persons who invite you for a meal. One of them is addicted to ostentation, and is fond of amusement; they invite you with kind words.

The other has a simple life, content with little; they invite you to a simple soup, without using flattering words. It is the time of offering the Prayer.

You accept the first invitation, which is very rich, abandon performing the Prayer in congregation and its Sunna part; you may even accept it at the cost of abandoning the Prayer entirely.

However, you do not accept the other, simple invitation and prefer to do the Prayer with its Sunna part, which gives spiritual delight and lasting pleasure.

The first invitation represents the present civilization, while the other, the popular civilization, is more equitable.

Pure justice issues from Islam and gives life to the spirit. It does not destroy your life; the life it offers is free of wrong and therefore of darkness. It leads to perfect truth.

Muslims have learnt a lesson; due to their neglect and heedlessness, Islam has resented them. While Christians – making friends with civilization and science in a deceptive way and appropriating these – have prevailed over us.

Now an awesome weapon is being manufactured in the East; its completion is near at hand. It is for the most part truth, which is our property, and therefore we must protect it. As for its deceitful, varnished part, we must leave it to its manufacturers.

If we remain indifferent to it, and feel resentful against it, as we did in the past, Christendom will make friends with it and use it against us to the detriment of Islam. It will be very difficult to resist.

It is a new idea, both calamitous and useful, which is turned toward the public. If an idea addressed to the public does not acquire sacredness, it will soon decline and die.

There are two great religions which provide an idea with sacredness, but one will bring darkness upon it, while the other, light.

This astute Eastern idea – when it was born, it discovered that the present Christianity was its enemy, standing right beside it. So, it never made peace with the religion.

This idea or way surely needs permanence and its permanence depends on its acceptance by the public.

Acceptance by the public requires that there is sacredness. That which can give it sacredness must be a religion that considers the public mercifully.

This means that this idea or way will inevitably resort to Islam, or it will die; it must be well aware of this.

If you say, "Why is it that Islam has grown wretched and outlandish, losing its glory, and we have sunk together, along with the prosperity it gave us? The star of Islam is not yet on the rise."

I say in reply: "It has happened so because we have fallen in love with the West and turned to it with an inauspicious love."

We have caused the sun of Islam to set. When we turn our faces to the east in earnest, it is then that the glory of Islam will illuminate the moon. It will receive its light from the sun of Islam and scatter it, and the crescent of Islam will rise high.

We have been deceived and we have committed great errors, spending our love abroad and spreading hostility at home. We must come to our senses so that we may recover and develop.

The answer to the Anglican Church

Once a fierce, pitiless enemy of Islam, a political intriguer, a scheming deceiver who desired to show themselves as superior, in the guise of a priest, with the intention of denial,

At a grievous time, squeezing our throat with its claws, they asked us four things in a spiteful manner, wanting us to answer in six hundred words.

We should have responded by spitting in the face of such spitefulness, and by keeping silent in resentment in the face of their intrigue, and by giving a silencing, resounding answer to their denial.

However, I will not stoop to speak to that enmity, but will give the following answer to a truth-seeking one:

The truth-seeking one asked: "What is the religion which Muhammad brought?" I answered:

"It is contained in the Qur'an. The basic purposes of the Qur'an are the six pillars of belief and the five pillars of Islamic life."

His second question was: "What has it given to human thought and life?" I answered: "It has given unity to human thought and a straight direction to life. My witnesses to this are:

> *Say: "He, (He is) God, (Who is) the Unique One of absolute Oneness"* (112:1), *and Pursue, then, what is exactly right as you are commanded* (11:112).

He also asked: "How does it heal the present diseases of humanity?" I answered: "Through the ban on interest and usury, and the obligation of *Zakah*. My witnesses to this are:

> *God deprives interest and usury of any blessing* (2:176); *God has made trading lawful and interest and usury unlawful* (2:275); *Establish the Prayer and pay the Zakah (the Prescribed Purifying Alms)* (2:43).

Fourthly, he asked: "How does it view the tumults and revolutions in humanity?" I said in reply:

"Labor is essential, and wealth cannot be accumulated or held only in the hands of the rich and oppressors. My witnesses to this are:

> *Man has only that for which he labors* (53:39); *Those who hoard up gold and silver and do not spend it in God's cause (to exalt His cause and help the poor and needy): give them the glad tidings of a painful punishment* (9:34).

Rather than the general gravity, it is the spiritual gravity of the Qur'an which preserves our globe

It is this heavenly rope which holds our earth and rotates it around its daily and yearly axes. It anchors the earth securely, and is mounted on it, preventing it from rebelling.

The Shari'a descended from God's Supreme Throne and caused a luminous worship to rise from humankind. Of worship, the five daily Prayers and the calls to Prayer recited before it

Are bound together, one after the other. These five luminous ropes have bound humanity and the earth both with the realm of the Unseen and the Divine Supreme Throne.

These connecting bonds, the starting point of which are the five daily Prayers, and the end point of which are the Divine Throne and the

Unseen, connect the corporeal, visible realm with the Unseen, the earth with humankind, and humankind with the heavens.

These five bonds are a belt around the earth, made up of five belts; both separate and connected to one another. They are also its garment, the two poles being the arms; earth's inhabitants are never left naked.

These belts become united in a single instant, resembling the light of the sun. They are at the same time separate, like the luminous bands of rainbow, and

At a single point they are both connected to the Divine Throne and connect the earth to the Divine Throne. They impart life to the earth, rotating it. If this garment is torn,

Or if one of the ropes is severed, watch the uproar! The darkness of cold weighs down on it heavily, and it freezes; this indicates the imminence of its death and the destruction of the world: an utterly terrible tremor.

Assuredly We have honored the children of Adam (17:70).

Someone asked: "Why is it that only humankind has been honored with the supreme rank – to undertake the Supreme Trust – and made vice-gerent on the earth?"

I said in answer: The best of things is that which is in the middle and moderate. If a cone is drawn in the center of the universe, from side to side, the atom is at its pointed end.

At the center point of the luminous diameter of the universe, which extends as far as the sun of the suns, is humanity, standing and protecting the Supreme Trust.

The distances between the atom and humanity and between humanity and the sun are of the same length. Humankind is a unique link in the necklace of creation.

For that unique gem is a pleasant shell for the pearl orphan, the Prophet Muhammadu'l-Hashimi, upon him be peace and blessings; it is a miniature sample of the whole of creation, which encapsulates the Unseen and the visible world.

It has windows, each opening onto a world; it looks at these worlds through these windows. In addition to its inner and outer senses, it has many other senses.

Like smell and taste, motive or urge is also a sense, as is enthusiasm. Both are very subtle, not dependent on reason or sight, and have many places to travel.

They – motive and enthusiasm – hold in their hands many things perceived through presentiment, true dreams, and sound spiritual discovery or illumination.

Thinking that the covering is the essence means losing the essence

Five things curtain five other things: the visible corporeal realm curtains the Unseen; nature, the Divine Will; blind force, Divine Power; the word, the inferred meaning; and the meaning inferred, the meaning itself.

Concentration on the curtain always leads to error and gives rise to groundless suspicions. For example, the meaning inferred: its place is the mind and it entertains the intelligence.

Preoccupation with and concentration on the meaning formed in the mind leads to deviation from the meaning itself, and to a form that is lifeless and infertile.

This weak, unproductive activity consumes energy and effort, and its output is a form of no use, which neither justifies the effort and energy, nor satisfies one's enthusiasm, nor pleases one's sense of delight.

Therefore, the meaning inferred should either be made transparent or holes should be made in it so that it is open onto the outer world and to the activity of the intelligence.

For the outer world is broad, a place where hearts and minds are active, and it comprises established realities. The shirt which you have sewn, like a spider's web, from a part of the meaning in your narrow mind –

Do not attempt to place that shirt – which is too tight for a fly – on the Supreme Seat and Throne of God. On the page of the meaning that you infer in your mind you have drawn a tiny map, as tiny as a the wing of a fly, but as roomy as the capital city for holding suspicions,

Then you lose yourself in that tiny, fragile space and desire to gallop across it. What a calamity that is!

O materialist, naturalist one, blinded by force and deceived by forms and words. Give up following the scientifically materialist genius so that you can rise to right guidance.

Out of the five curtains I have indicated only one as an example; it is the least of the five, so compare others to it. The fallacies of materialism lead you into hellish pits.

Instead, hold fast to the chain that raises the soul to the heavens. It raises us high into Paradise.

Prayer should not be made for something impossible and should not contain sinful words

Any prayer made sincerely is absolutely accepted; whatever is asked for is given either as asked for or in some other way. But there are some conditions and one who prays should always assume the required manner of asking from God.

Without the required good manners, neither prayers nor any other act of worship will be accepted.

One cannot assume a manner of complaining about God or reproving Him in prayer; nor can one pray whimsically and capriciously.

Anything impossible or contrary to Divine wisdom and the Divine order of the universe should not be asked for.

One cannot also ask for infinitude concerning something finite. Saying, "Make me attain the highest of goals!" is a fantasy that acknowledges no limits, and is not a prayer that requires modesty or entreaty.

Likewise, fixing an amount, saying, for example: "to the numbers of the things in God's Knowledge," is not suited to prayer –

Unless one means abundance by that amount. However, one cannot always bear intention in mind while praying.

Part Three

Part Three

Arguments on the Condition of Muslims and How to Improve It

The diseases from which Muslims suffer and their cures

HAVE BEEN STUDYING AT THE UNIVERSITY OF HUMAN SOCIAL LIFE AT the present time, and come to realize that while the Europeans are flying high into the future in material progress, the follow-ing six obstacles have kept us in the middle ages in respect of material development:

The *first* is the revival of despair within us.

The *second* is the death of truthfulness and honesty in political and social life.

The *third* is loving hostility.

The *fourth* is the ignorance of the spiritual bonds that connect the believers to one another.

The *fifth* is oppression that spreads throughout all aspects of life like a contagious disease.

The *sixth* is the restriction of exertions to personal interests.

I will explain the cures for these six terrible diseases in our social life with the six words I have received from the pharmacy of the Qur'an, which is like a school of medicine.

The cures

THE FIRST WORD OR CURE IS HOPE AND ASPIRATION

That is, we should have strong hope and unshakeable confidence in God's Mercy. Based on the lesson I have learned, O Muslim community, I give the glad tidings and pronounce with such certainty as to make the whole world hear that the future will be Islam's exclusively. For all the truths of Islam have the innate ability to develop both materially and spiritually. History, which records events in the human realm, is the most truthful witness of this truth. It shows us – as professed by the Japanese commander who defeated the Russians – that the Muslims have progressed to the extent of their adherence to the truths of Islam and have derived their power from the strength of these truths, while they have declined to the extent of their weakness in following them. The reverse of this reality is true for other religions. Their followers have progressed to the extent of their weakness in adherence to their religions and suffered revolutions and decline in proportion to their attachment.

No period of history, from the Age of Happiness until now, tells us that a Muslim has preferred another religion over Islam with their sound reasoning and entered that religion based on sound proof. It is true that there have been some who have left Islam; but this has been through imitation and is of no importance. However, the followers of other religions – even some from among the British and Russians, who are most attached to their religion – have continuously entered the fold of Islam in throngs based on sound proof and through sound reasoning. If we demonstrate through our acts the perfections of Islamic morality and the truth of Islam, the followers of other religions will continue to enter it in greater numbers; even some entire regions and countries of the earth will accept it.

Moreover, humankind has awakened through the warning of sciences, wars and other terrible events, and has come to comprehend the true nature of humanity and perceived its comprehensive capacity. So people cannot be human and live without religion. The irreligious among humanity have been obliged to take refuge in religion. For our only point of reliance and support in the face of our essential weakness and the wounds of external hostilities and calamities, and our only point of seeking help in the face of our essential poverty and limitless needs and desires that extend toward eternity is the recognition of the Maker of the universe, and believing in and confirming Him and the Hereafter.

Humanity has also come to understand that with such a comprehensive essence, they have not been created for this brief, tumultuous worldly life. They are destined for an eternal life; they have desires and tendencies that extend toward eternity. Everyone has come to feel that the fleeting, narrow world is not sufficient for the realization of our limitless desires and aspirations. If the power of imagination, which is a servant of humanity, is told, "You will be given a million years of life as the king of all humankind but you will finally be executed for eternity, without revival," the imaginative faculty of one who has not lost their true humanity will utter sighs of regret and weep for the non-existence of an eternal life of happiness.

It is for these most substantial realities that everyone has begun to perceive a tendency deep in their heart to seek a true religion. First of all, they are seeking a truth in the true religion on which they can rely against the execution of death, so that they may save themselves.

In short, we Muslims, who are the students of the Qur'an, follow proof and accept the truths of belief with our reason, intellect, and heart. Unlike some members of other religions, we do not abandon proof and blindly imitate religious leaders. Therefore, in the future, when reason, sciences, and knowledge will dominate, it will be the Qur'an, the decrees and propositions of which are all confirmed by reason, that will certainly rule.

THE EIGHT OBSTACLES BEFORE ISLAM'S FULL DOMINION IN THE PAST

The following eight obstacles prevented the truths of Islam from thoroughly invading the continent of the past:

The first, second and third of these obstacles were the ignorance of the Europeans, their distance from civilization, and their bigoted attachment to their religion. These three obstacles are being destroyed through scientific developments and the virtues of civilization.

The fourth and fifth obstacles were the domination of priests and religious leaders, and the people's blind imitation of them. These two obstacles began to be removed through the birth of the freedom of thought and a tendency toward searching for the truth.

The sixth and seventh obstacles were oppression in us and our bad morals which arise from our opposition to the Shari'a. The decline of personal, political oppression gives the glad tidings that the terrible oppressions of a society or class or a committee will also come to an end within thirty or forty years.[52] In addition to this, the outburst of Islamic zeal and the realization of the evil results of bad morals will cause the disappearance of these obstacles. They are disappearing and, God willing, will disappear completely.

The eighth obstacle is the misunderstanding that the established facts of sciences are contrary to the outer meaning of some Islamic truths. For example, the two angels called *Thawr* (Ox) and *Hut* (Fish) have been taken to mean a huge, physical ox and fish respectively, and the people of science and philosophy, unaware of the truth of the matter, have opposed Islam.[53] There are many other examples like this one which even the most obstinate opponents have felt obliged to accept the truth of them after having come to understand them.[54] So, the studies of some verifying Muslim scholars to explain such matters signal that this eighth, terrible obstacle will be utterly destroyed.

Equipped with sciences, knowledge, and the virtues of civilization, the human tendency to seek the truth, fairness and the feeling of justice in human nature, as well as love of humanity, are beginning to defeat and remove the above-mentioned eight obstacles. God willing, these obstacles will be utterly demolished within half a century. It is with complete certainty that I announce: Europe and America are pregnant with Islam and will give birth to a Muslim state one day in the future, just as the Ottomans are pregnant with Europe and will give birth to a European state (and so they did).

THE FIVE POWERS THAT REINFORCE MUSLIMS

The truths of Islam have also the innate ability to develop materially and therefore Islam will rule in the future, for five strong, unbreakable powers have been united and fused.[55]

---

[52]   39 years after this sermon by Said Nursi, which he gave in 1911 in Damascus, the single party domination ended and multi-party democracy began in Turkey. (Tr.)

[53]   Said Nursi explained this matter in *Muhakemat*, published in English as *The Reasonings*, Tughra Books, New Jersey 2008, pp. 54–56. (Tr.)

[54]   Said Nursi also dealt with some of these matters in *The Reasonings*. (Tr.)

[55]   We understand from the teaching of the Qur'an that with the mention of the miracles of the Prophets the Qur'an informs us that humankind will imitate them and develop, and encourages us to do so. It says:

The first power is the truth of Islam, the teacher of all perfections, which is able to unite hundreds of millions of souls into one soul, and equipped with true civilization and sciences, and which is so strong that no force can break it.

The second is the intense neediness, the true master of civilization and crafts, and which is equipped with the completion of the prerequisites and means of development, and our poverty, which almost breaks our backs. This is such a force that it cannot be silenced or defeated.

The third power is the freedom ordered and allowed by the Shari'a. It urges humankind to race for the attainment of lofty goals, smashes oppression, and invigorates elevated feelings. At the present, this power is equipped with competition, awakening, vigilance, the zeal of competing, and a tendency toward revival and civilization. In short, it is equipped with the tendency toward and desire for the loftiest perfections that are most fitting for humankind.

The fourth is courage and the spirit of enterprise that results from belief and which is equipped with compassion. That is, it is not lowering oneself before injustices or wrongdoers, and it is not degrading the oppressed. As a foundation of the freedom that is encouraged by the Shari'a, this fourth power means not flattering oppressors and not domineering over the weak and poor.

The fifth power is Islamic dignity. It requires the uplifting of God's Name. At this time, uplifting God's Name depends on material development and the adoption of true civilization. It cannot be doubted that in

---

Work and display the examples of these miracles! Like Prophet Solomon, upon him be peace, cover a distance of two months within one day; like Prophet Jesus, upon him be peace, try to cure the most terrible diseases; like the Staff of Prophet Moses, upon him be peace, extract the water of life from rocks and save humankind from thirst; like Prophet Abraham, upon him be peace, discover the substances which will save you from fire and don them; like some Prophets, upon them be peace, hear the most distant voices in the east and west, and see the most distant forms; like Prophet David, upon him be peace, melt iron like dough or make it like wax so that it may be used as a means for all technical developments; and as much as you benefit from the clock and ship, which were the miracles of Prophets Joseph and Noah respectively, upon them be peace, benefit from all the miracles of other Prophets, and imitate them. (For a detailed explanation of this matter by Said Nursi, see *The Words* (trans.), "The 20th Word," The Light, New Jersey 2005, pp. 59–79. [Tr.])

Teaching humankind in every respect in order to urge them to spiritual and material development, the Qur'an demonstrates that it is a universal teacher.

the future the collective persona of the world of Islam will completely ful-fill this duty, which the dignity of Islam requires based on belief.

Islam has sometimes had to resort to the sword in the past in order to break the bigotry and obstinacy of the enemy, and repel its attack. But in the future, it will defeat its enemies with true civilization, material devel-opment, and the spiritual sword of truth and right.

Understand what follows:

What we demand in the name of civilization is its beauty and its good aspects, which are beneficial for humankind. We never demand its vices or evils, which some fools regard as beauty and which have destroyed our own "wealth" by our imitation. They have bribed the world in return for the Religion, but they have not been able to take the world. The vices of civilization have overcome its beauties and humanity has received a terri-ble blow (now two terrible blows) in the form of a world war and has thus stained the world with blood. God willing, supported by the power of Islam, the beauties of civilization will prevail in the future, clean the earth of filth, and secure general peace.

Since the tendency toward perfection is ingrained in human nature, if humanity does not suffer total destruction due to its faults and injustices, the truth of Islam will bring happiness to the Muslim world in particular, and the whole world in general, and will thus serve as atonement for the past and present vices of humanity.

Look, time does not move in a straight line so that its beginning and end grow distant from one another. Rather, like the movement of the earth, time moves by drawing a circle. It sometimes displays progress as an embodiment of spring and summer and sometimes displays decline as an embodiment of winter and a season of storms. So, just as every winter is followed by spring and every night by the morning, so too humankind will, God willing, also live a new morning and spring. From the Divine Mercy we can expect to see the true civilization marked by a general peace in the sun of the truth of Islam.

Furthermore, as scientific studies and uncountable experiences clear-ly show, what is dominant in the order of the universe and in the basic purposes of the All-Majestic Maker for its existence are good, beauty, and perfection. For every branch of science that studies the universe indicates such a magnificent order and perfection with the general principles on which it is based that minds cannot conceive of something better than this universe. For example, the sciences of anatomy, astronomy, botany, and zoology, with the general principles of being the direct result of the order of the All Majestic Creator, display His miracles of Power and Wisdom, as well as the truth of *He Who makes excellent everything that He creates* (32:7).

It is also an observable and experienced fact that evil, ugliness, falsehood, and badness are secondary and subordinate in creation. They are not the purposes of creation; rather, they exist indirectly and as measures of comparison. For example, ugliness serves for beauty to be manifested in various forms and degrees. Evil, and even Satan, have been allowed to attack humans so that they may function as a means for the development and perfection of human beings. In short, ugliness and evil have been created to serve as means for universal beauty and good.

Good, perfection, and beauty are essential to the existence of the universe. So, humankind, who has sullied the earth with its injustices and unbelief, will not be able to go to non-existence without first suffering the punishment for such atrocities and then without being the means for the realization of the basic purposes for the existence of the universe (by observing the Divine order).

It is another established fact that humankind is the noblest and most important among creatures. For humankind is a unit of comparison to understand the acts and Art of God. It discovers with its intellect the relationship and steps between the apparent causes and their effects in the creation and operation of the universe, and thus imitates the wise acts and works of God's Art. It also acquires knowledge of God's Art, His universal, all-encompassing acts, and His Attributes through its particular knowledge and artistry. All this proves that humankind is the most honorable and noblest creature in the universe.

Also, as testified by the truths of Islam that pertain to the universe and humankind, the people of Islam, who are the people of truth, are the most distinguished and honorable among human beings. As demonstrated by history and attested to by the almost one thousand miracles of Prophet Muhammad and by his most exalted morality and best conduct, as well as the truths of the Qur'an and Islam, Prophet Muhammad, upon him be peace and blessings, is the most blessed and the highest of the people of Islam and therefore of humankind.[56]

In the face of these realities, is it possible that humankind can contradict the testimonies of science, history, experiences, and logic and thus resist the Divine Will and Wisdom, Which encompass the whole universe? Can it continue its savageries, obstinate unbelief, and terrible destruction? Is it at all possible that the present state, which is contrary to Islam, can last?

I swear with all my strength, and I wish I could swear with countless tongues by the All-Majestic, the All-Gracious and All-Beautiful Maker, Who has created this universe from particles to planets, from the wings of flies to the lamps of the heavens with perfect wisdom, that contrary to all other species of creation and all the varieties of existent beings that are inferior to it, humankind will not be able to oppose the universal order with its universal evils much longer; it will not be able to continue eating and digesting the Hellish fruits of the triumph of evil over good in its realm. So, just as the existence of Paradise and Hell is certain, so too, the future victory of good and the true Religion is beyond question; thus will humankind be equal to its brothers and sisters – all other species – in the universe in the domination of good and virtue, and thus will the mystery of the eternal Wisdom be realized in the human realm as well.

If the evils and injustices of humankind do not soon cause Doomsday to burst on the head of humankind, we entreat the Mercy of the All-Merciful and the All-Compassionate to make the truths of Islam a means for the salvation of humankind from falling to the lowest of the low, for the purification of the earth of its sins, and the realization of universal peace.

THE SECOND WORD OR CURE

Is what follows, and it is to this that my life-experiences have given rise:

Despair is a most terrible disease which has infiltrated into the heart of the Muslim world. It is despair which has killed us and caused a small Western state of a few millions to dominate tens of millions of Muslims in the east and to colonize their country. It is also despair which has extin-

---

[56]   For the excellences of the miracles of Prophet Muhammad, upon him be peace and blessings, see Said Nursi, *The Letters* (trans.), "The 19th Letter," The Light, New Jersey 2007, pp. 117–236. (Tr.)

guished our elevated morals and led us to abandon public interest and restrict our views to our personal interests. It is despair which has ruined our spiritual and moral power to such an extent that while our earlier generations, who were small in number but equipped with extraordinary spiritual and moral power, conquered a vast area that stretched from the east to the west, unjust foreigners have captured and reduced to slavery hundreds of millions of Muslims for the last four centuries. Those Muslims have found a pretext for their laziness in one another's indifference and loss of energy, saying, "Everyone is bad like me," and abandoned Islamic zeal and the responsibility to serve Islam, which is required by belief. Since this disease has done us such wrong and almost kills us, we will, God willing, smash its head with *Do not despair of God's Mercy* (39:53), and break its waist with the truth of the Islamic principle, "If something cannot be obtained entirely, it is not to be abandoned entirely."

Despair is the most terrible disease, a cancer, for nations. It blocks the way to perfection and is contrary to the truth of God's pronouncement, "I am with my servant in the way he thinks of Me."[57] It is the characteristic of the ignoble, cowardly, and impotent. It can never be at one with Islamic valor and the spirit of endeavor. God willing, all Muslim peoples will go hand in hand with each other in perfect solidarity and unity, and hoist the flag of the Qur'an all over the world.

THE THIRD WORD OR CURE

All my studies during my life and the social tumult I have witnessed have informed me that truthfulness is the very foundation of Islam, the bond that connects all its elevated characteristics with one another, and the essence and sum of lofty feelings. Therefore, we should revive truthfulness as the foundation of our social life and cure our spiritual diseases with it.

Truthfulness is the core of Islamic social life. Ostentation is a deceitful act; sycophancy and pretension are a very mean kind of lying. Hypocrisy is a most harmful kind of lying. Lying is slandering the Power of the All-Majestic Maker.

---

[57]   al-Bukhari, "Tawhid" 15; Muslim, "Tawba" 2, at-Tirmidhi, "Zuhd" 51.

With all its kinds, unbelief is a lie, while belief is truthfulness. For this reason, there is an infinite distance between lying and truthfulness, so they must be kept infinitely far from each other; they can never exist together. However, merciless politics and unjust propaganda have combined them, and thus confused human perfection.[58]

Truthfulness and lies are as far apart from one another as belief and unbelief. Prophet Muhammad, upon him be peace and blessings, rose to the highest of the high through truthfulness and opened with this the treasures of the truths of belief and the truths of the universe or creation, while Musaylima the Liar,[59] and those like him, fell into the lowest of the low through lying. For this reason, truthfulness has been the most valued and desired property in the marketplace of human social life. This is why the Prophet's Companions never knowingly became customers of lies or sullied themselves with falsehoods. Since they always sought truthfulness, with all their strength, in the footsteps of Prophet Muhammad, upon him be peace and blessings, their justice and truthfulness became a standard in the science of Hadith. The scholars of the Hadith and Shari'a concluded that the narrations from the holy Prophet made by these heroes were true and reliable.

---

[58]   O brothers and sisters! The Old or Former Said was involved in politics and Islamic social life. But never think that he followed the way of using the Religion as an instrument for politics. God forbid! Rather, he did his utmost to be able to use politics as an instrument for the Religion. He used to say: "I prefer a single truth of the Religion over worldly politics." Through a premonition he felt that some hypocritical heretics would use politics as an instrument for irreligion, and so the Old Said tried with all strength to make politics serve the Religion.

However, twenty years later the Old Said saw that while those hypocritical heretics were using politics as an instrument for irreligion on the pretext of Westernization, some religious politicians attempted to use the Religion as an instrument for Islamic politics. The sun of Islam cannot be put under the service of the stars of the earth. Using it in the service of these stars means reducing the value of Islam and this is a great crime. The Old Said eventually saw to what point politics might even take religious people. He witnessed that due to political bias a pious, righteous scholar highly praised a hypocrite who shared his political stance, while he criticized and accused of transgression a righteous learned man who opposed his political views. The Old Said said to him: "If a devil supports you in your political stance, you would call God's blessing on him; but if an angel came and opposed you, you would curse him." Consequently, the Old Said said, "I seek refuge in God from Satan and politics," and gave up political involvement completely.

[59]   Musaylima (the Liar) was a person who claimed Prophethood after Prophet Muhammad, upon him be peace and blessings. (Tr.)

While with the lofty revolution that took place in the Age of Happiness truthfulness and lies and belief and unbelief were infinitely distant from each other, they have come nearer to one another over time. Political propaganda has sometimes made lying something that is desirable, and thus evil and lying have spread to a certain extent. It is for this reason that no one now can attain the level of the Companions.

As for lying for possible benefits, time has abrogated this. The present time has annulled the permission which some scholars gave to lie temporarily for a certain acceptable benefit. For this permission has been misused so frequently that if it enables one benefit, its harm is a hundredfold.

Whatever you say must be true, but it may not be right to speak out every truth recklessly. If saying a truth will cause harm, one must keep silent, but never attempt to tell lies. Whatever you say must be right, but you have no right to say everything that is right. For if you are not sincere in saying it, it may cause an evil result, and thus right comes to serve wrong.

THE FOURTH WORD OR CURE

What is most fitting for and worthy of love is love, and what is most worthy of hostility is hostility. That is, the attribute of love, which enables a happy human social life, most deserves love; while hostility, which ruins human social life, is an ugly, harmful attribute most deserving of hostility and hatred.

The time of hostility has come to an end. The two world wars have shown how evil and devastatingly wrong hostility can be. It is manifestly clear that evil has not the least benefit for humankind. For this reason, unless evil acts are in the form of aggression, such acts on the part of our enemies should not drive us to hostility. Hell or God's punishment is enough for them.

Arrogance and selfishness sometimes wrongly lead believers to feel hostility toward their brothers or sisters-in-religion. Even though they may see themselves as rightful, hostility toward believers means belittling the powerful reasons for loving them, such as belief, being Muslim, and a fellow human. This is paramount to lunacy; preferring the pebble-sized reasons for hostility over mountain-sized reasons of love. That is, the reasons for love are the luminous, powerful chains and the spiritual castles such as belief, being Muslim, and being human, while the reasons for hostility toward believers are no more than pebbles. Therefore, hostility toward believers is as great a wrong as disparaging the mountain-like reasons for love.

In short: Brother/sisterhood and love are the characteristics of Islam and of bonds between Muslims. The people of hostility are like mischievous children, who desire to cry and therefore seek a reason to cry. They make a thing that is as petty as the wing of a fly a pretext for crying. They are also like an unfair, pessimistic man who does not have a good opinion of others as long as it is possible to have an ill opinion. He covers ten instances or acts of good with a single evil. As Islamic characteristics, fairness and the rule of having a good opinion of others counter this attitude.

THE FIFTH WORD OR CURE

What follows is a lesson I have learned from Islamic consultation:

At the present time one sin does not remain one; it grows and infects others, multiplying many times over. Similarly, a good act does not remain single; it sometimes grows by thousands of degrees. This is due to the following:

Islamic freedom and consultation have demonstrated the dominion of our true nationality. The foundation and spirit of our true nationality is Islam. Muslim peoples, including in particular the Turks and Arabs, are shells or citadels of this nationality.

Through the bond of this sacred nationality all Muslims are like a single tribe. Like the members of a tribe, Muslim peoples are connected to one another in Islamic brother/sisterhood. They support each other spiritually and, when necessary, materially. It is as if all Muslim peoples are connected to each other with a luminous chain. So, consider this: if a member of a tribe commits a crime, in the sight of an enemy tribe all the members of the tribe are to blame, and that single crime has the effect of thousands of crimes. If a member of the tribe does something good, which will bring honor to the entire tribe, all members of the tribe take pride in him, as if each member had earned this glory.

It is due to this reality that an evil committed does not remain restricted to the one who commits it. It may be a transgression against the rights of millions of Muslims. The clearer examples of this will be seen in forty or fifty years of time.

So, O brothers, who are listening to me in this Umayyad Mosque and Muslim brothers and sisters in the future mosque of the Muslim world! Do not offer excuses, saying, "We are not doing harm, and we are unable to do good, thus we are excused." This excuse of yours is not acceptable. Your laziness, indifference, and lack of effort through Islamic nationality and unity are a great harm and a wrong on your part.

Like an evil multiplying thousands of times over, any good done at this time pertaining to the sacredness of Islam will never remain restricted to the one who does it. It may be beneficial for millions of believers. It may strengthen the bond of the spiritual and material life. Therefore, it is not time to remain indifferent (to the problems of Muslims and what is going on around us), or to fall onto the bed of laziness. The benefit and worldly and otherworldly happiness of small Muslim nationalities, such as the Kurds, are dependent upon the great peoples such as the Turks and Arabs. We suffer harm because of your indolence and loss of zeal and energy. For this reason, the sin you commit through laziness is very great. The good you will do will also be great and exalted. With my defective understanding, I see the social body of Muslims as a factory with a number of wheels. If one of these wheels stops or works more slowly than others or interferes with another wheel, the order and functionality of the factory are upset. So we should ignore each other's personal faults.

Just as some of the Europeans have taken our valuable properties and lands from us and have given in return a very insignificant, inadequate price, so too have they taken from us some of our elevated moral values and some of our lofty characteristics in social life. They have used these as a means for their development and in return given us their vices and evil characteristics.

For example, due to a national characteristic they have borrowed from us, one of them says, "Even if I die, let my nation survive, for I have a permanent life in my nation." They have borrowed this lofty characteristic from us and made a most formidable foundation for their development. This characteristic issues from the true Religion and truths of belief. It belongs to the people of belief. Whereas due to an evil characteristic which has come to us from foreigners, a selfish man from among us says,

"If I die of thirst, let rain no more come down on the world. If I cannot be happy, let the world become corrupted in whatever way it will." This foolish, evil attitude issues from irreligion; it comes from ignorance of the Hereafter. It has entered us from abroad and poisons us. A person from Europe gains as much value as their nation due to their national and patriotic zeal. For a man is valuable to the extent of their intentions and endeavors. Whoever lives and endeavors for the happiness of their nation is a nation by themselves.

Despite our sacred Islamic nationality, because of either heedlessness or the influence of evil characteristics we have borrowed from abroad, a person cares only about themselves and pursues their personal interests, indifferent to the common interests of the nation. Thus, a thousand people are reduced to the level of a single person. Whoever pursues only their personal interests cannot be counted as a human being, because humans are civilized by nature; a human being is obliged to care about their fellow human beings. Their personal life can continue within social life. For example, in order to obtain a loaf of bread, one needs the cooperation of numerous hands. You can compare to bread the clothes one wears. A person cannot live with skin like animals and therefore they have to be interrelated with their fellow human beings. One who restricts themselves to their personal interests is no longer a human being; they have been reduced to a cannibalistic animal.

THE SIXTH WORD OR CURE

The key to the happiness of Muslims in social life is consultation, as ordered by the Shari'a. The verse, *Their affairs are by consultation among themselves* (42:38) orders consultation as a basis of social life and administration. While the consultation between eras in human history under the name: "the opinions supporting one another over time" has been a propitious ground for scientific and technical development, the abandonment of consultation is one of the reasons for the regression in Asia.

The key to the happy future of Asia is consultation. Like consultation among individuals, countries should consult with one another so that the fetters of various sorts of oppression placed around the feet of hundreds of thousands of Muslims will be removed. The consultation ordered by the

Shari'a and the freedom established by the Shari'a, born of the compassion and zeal that originate in belief and are decorated with the good manners ordered by the Shari'a – it is this consultation and freedom that will remove the fetters of all the oppression that are clamped around the feet of Muslims; only in this way can we discard the evils and vices borrowed from modern Western civilization. Islamic freedom, which is based on belief, orders the following two things: degrading no one through oppression and disallowing oneself to be degraded through bowing to oppressors. Whoever becomes a true servant of God never admits servitude to others. *None of us should take others for lords, apart from God* (3:64). One who does not recognize God or become His servant conceives a kind of lordship in all others, each according to their status and sets others over themselves. By contrast, the freedom established by the Shari'a is a gift from God as a manifestation of His being the All-Merciful and the All-Compassionate, and it is a characteristic of belief.

Consultation results in sincerity and solidarity and causes three separate ones (1-1-1) to become one hundred and eleven (111). Thus, through sincerity and solidarity, three persons may be as beneficial for the nation as more than one hundred people. Many historical incidents inform us that through the sincerity and solidarity that result from consultation, ten persons give as great a service as a thousand people. Since humankind suffers from limitless needs and innumerable hostility but has insignificant power and capital, and particularly, as it is threatened by people of destruction who have turned into brutal creatures through irreligion, humanity can resist them only by discovering the points of reliance and help through belief, and only thus, through consultation, can social life continue.

We Easterners are not like Westerners. The emergence of the Prophets in the east and the appearance of philosophers mostly in the West is a message of Divine Destiny, informing us that it is religious endeavor and zeal that will awaken the East and urge it to develop. Religious zeal and endeavor should be given priority and national zeal and endeavor should support it. Religious zeal and endeavor is a luminous, unbreakable chain that extends from the Divine Throne; it is an indestructible castle. History is a witness to this.

One of the most terrible calamities visiting us is belittling religious scholars, an attitude which we have borrowed from Westerners. In fact, religious scholars are more worthy of respect, compassion, and love than any other people. The faults and defects attributed to them do not arise from their existence; they arise from a lack of perfect, verifying scholars due to the problems of the time. Religious scholars are the supports of Islamic life.

I once heard that someone noticed that the pillar under his roof had weakened. Before putting in a new, powerful pillar, this man began to remove the other one. As a consequence, the roof collapsed on his head.

I have also witnessed that in order to set forth a proof for the glory and greatness of the Caliph 'Umar, may God be pleased with him, someone said that 'Umar was as tall as a minaret. When another one warned him that 'Umar's height was an allusion to his personal virtues and grandeur in spirit, the other man said: "In that case, 'Umar was an ordinary one like us."

I also observed that a man was attacking another's steadfastness in religion to condemn bigotry. But since he did not mention or emphasize that this person's steadfastness in religion lay in his piety, righteousness, morality, and regularity in the practice of religion, and as he did not draw attention to these virtues, by criticizing a man of steadfastness in religion and reducing his value in people's sight, he actually attacked the virtuous attribute of steadfastness in religion itself and reduced it in people's estimation.

So, whoever wants to displace the weak pillar under the roof of their house let them first put in a new, strong pillar and make the house safe. Otherwise, they will destroy their house unwittingly.

A person who wants to falsify and annul an unsound argument that is put forth to support a truth should first support that truth with a sound proof. Otherwise, they will unwittingly falsify the truth.

A person who wants to attack bigotry should first establish steadfastness in the religion, taking it under protection and emphasizing its virtue and value. Otherwise, they will unwillingly mislead others.

(From *Khutba-i Shamiya* ["The Sermon of Damascus"])

Two cardinal causes for Europe's development

There are two cardinal causes for the development and present dominion of Europe, one material, the other immaterial.

The first, material cause is the physical conditions of Europe, which is the "church" of all Christians and the source of their life. Europe is a narrow continent, "naturally" beautiful, has important rivers and vast sources of iron, is surrounded by seas on three sides, and has a meandering coastline.

Although Europe covers nearly one-fifteenth of the land on earth, it has attracted one-fourth (now nearly one-thirteenth) of the world population with its "natural" beauty and rich resources. It is a fact that the density of population is the cause of the multiplicity of need; the more people, the greater the need. Particularly when need increases, due to certain reasons such as traditions, modernism, or civilization, it cannot be satisfied through the "natural" productivity of the land. It is for this reason that need opens the way for new crafts, curiosity urges learning, and stress leads to dissipation.

A multiplicity of population gives rise to the invention of new crafts and an increase in learning. The narrowness of the European continent and the possibilities of travel and transportation via the seas and rivers have encouraged and facilitated tourism and mutual acquaintance, which in turn have led to continental trade. Mutual assistance or cooperation has resulted in partnership, mutual contact, and relations, which in turn have given rise to the exchange and development of views, while rivalry has brought about competition. In addition, since Europe is very rich in iron, which is the source of industry, iron has equipped its civilization with such a weapon that Europeans have plundered and usurped all the remnants of ancient civilizations throughout the world, thus destroying the balance of power in the world.

Furthermore, continental Europe is relatively cold, and this climate causes people to adopt everything late and abandon it late. This has gained Europeans firmness and steadfastness in their endeavors and caused their civilization to endure. Moreover, the formation of their states based on science, the constant collision between them, the hardships and harassment caused by their cruelly despotic systems, the pressure of the religious fanaticism, as represented by the Inquisition, which in turn has given birth to significant reactions, and the competition between the more modest elements have developed the capacities of Europeans and awakened in them certain meritorious tendencies and nationalism.

The second, immaterial cause is their point of reliance. When any Christian attempts to attain any of the successive or combined goals, they turn back and see a powerful point of reliance which lifts their morale. They find in themselves a power that will combat even the hardest and greatest of matters. An example of this point of reliance is the intriguing, sophisticated fanaticism of the Inquisition, which is ever ready to feed the roots of the life of many Christians and to cut off the life-veins of Muslims. Moreover, European civilization, which has been kneaded with materialistic irreligion, has become the barracks or church of a mass that has been armed with the intoxicating pride of the victory of their civilization.

(From Sünuhat ("Occurrences to the Heart"))

Why at this time are the Muslims poor?

QUESTION: In the past, we were rich and the non-Muslims were poor, but now everywhere it is the opposite case. Why?

ANSWER: Some incorrect suggestions and recommendations have destroyed the zeal to endeavor that is deduced from the Divine decree, *And that man has only that for which he labors* (53:40), and the Islamic teaching, "God loves one who works to earn their livelihood."

Some persons and preachers do not know that exalting God's Word at this time depends on material progress. They do not appreciate the world as the arable field of the Hereafter. They cannot distinguish between the requirements of the middle and later ages. They do not discriminate between the contentment with endeavor and what one already has, or the praiseworthy contentment with the result and wages that come after the full exertion of one's strength and possibilities. They confuse the two contrasting kinds of trust in God – one being a title to idleness and non-observance of the prerequisites for a desired result, which means resisting the balance between the means and labor and the result – a balance established by the Divine Will – and the other, required by Islam, which is the shell of true sincerity and means referring the outcome to Divine Will with full resignation after fulfilling all the prerequisites necessary to realize that outcome. They do not perceive the mystery of the Prophet's full concern and compassion for his community in saying: "My community! My Community!", nor can they comprehend the wisdom in the Prophetic saying: "The best of people are those who are the most useful and beneficial for people."[60] It is such people and preachers who have broken the inclination to and enthusiasm for labor and endeavor among the Muslims.

The second reason for our poverty is that we have sought government jobs and civil service posts for our livelihood, which is proportional to idleness and flatters pride.

The natural, dynamic way for livelihood is crafts, farming or agriculture, and trade. Civil service is the unnatural way. In my opinion, those who seek civil service and government jobs to secure a livelihood are impotent public beggars. One who seeks a civil service or administrative post should seek them only in order to serve the people and country – seeking them for livelihood means begging. Thus, since the civil service and government jobs have generally been in our hands, we have wasted our wealth and scattered our offspring around, losing both. However, the non-Muslims have kept crafts and trade in their hands, and thus become rich.

(From *Münazarat* ["Discussions"])

Despotism

QUESTION: What is despotism?

ANSWER: Despotism is oppression, domination, and arbitrary power. It is arbitrary treatment and compulsion based on violence. It is the unquestionable opinion of a single individual, and a ground suitable for all kinds of abuses. It is the foundation of injustice and destroys humanity. Despotism rolls humans down into the deepest of the valleys of misery and has caused the world of Islam to fall into humiliation and deprivation. It awakens personal grudges and hostilities, poisons Islam and infects everything with its poison. It has caused differences and disagreements between Muslims, as well as the birth of the schools of misguidance, such as the *Mu'tazila, Jabriyya,* and *Murji'a.*[61]

It is learned despotism – the father of imitation and the child of political despotism – which caused the birth of such sects as the *Mu'tazila, Jabriyya,* and *Murji'a,* which have so confused Muslims.

(From *Münazarat* ["Discussions"])

---

60   al-Munawi, *Faydu'l-Qadir,* 3:481.

61   *Murjci'a* is the school of creed which argues that if one has believed, no matter how sinful they are, God will forgive them and admit them into Paradise. (Tr.)

Getting out of the dungeon of inactivity

QUESTION: Why have we fallen into the dungeon of inactivity?

ANSWER: Life consists of endeavor; enthusiasm is its mount. When you ride upon enthusiasm and go out into the arena of life, you will first encounter despair, which is your severest enemy. It disheartens you. Combat this enemy with the sword of *Do not despair!* (39:53).

Then, the tyranny of the inclination to be superior to others, which is found in the arena of serving the truth (here, there is a free place for everyone who wants to serve) begins to attack. Striking endeavor on the head, it causes you to fall off your mount. Dispatch the truth of *Be and strive for God's sake only* against this enemy.

Afterwards, haste emerges and confuses the way by inciting you not to ascend all the steps, one by one, toward your goal. It prevents the endeavor from going further. Shield against this with: *Be patient, encourage each other to patience and help each other with it, and observe your duties in solidarity* (3:200).

Humans are civilized by nature, and are responsible for preserving the rights of their fellow-humans and living together with them to attain their due. However, after hastiness, the tendency toward isolation from others and individuality appears before you. Against this, dispatch the noble, altruistic warrior, *The best of people are those who are the most useful and beneficial for people.*

Then, customs find an opportunity in the laziness of others and attack you, making you immobile. Take refuge in the formidable castle of *Those who seek a point of reliance should rely on God only, not on others.*

Then comes the pitiless enemy of leaving the fulfillment of duties to one another, which arises from a lack of confidence in your way and impotence. Endeavor is prevented from any attempt. Elevate endeavor high to the peak of *Those who go astray can do you no harm if you yourselves are rightly guided* (5:105), so that the hand of that enemy cannot reach even the feet of endeavor.

Then comes the irreligious enemy that makes the fulfillment of a duty dependent upon absolute success, which means intervention in God's judgment and acts. It slaps endeavor in the face and punches it in the eye. Dispatch the dutiful truth of *Pursue what is right as you are commanded*

(11:112), and *Do not attempt to dominate your master,* so that endeavor learns its place.

Lastly comes the tendency to ease and comfort, the mother of all difficulties and the nest of all vices. This causes a loss of endeavor and casts you into the dungeon of deprivation and misery. Dispatch the noble warrior, *Man has only that for which he labors* (53:39) against this sorcerer. There is great ease in hardship, for the ease of an enthusiastic one lies only in strife and endeavor.

(From *Münazarat* ["Discussions"])

Constitutionalism

QUESTION: What is Constitutionalism?

ANSWER: I will not expound the Constitutionalism about which some officials, through their actions and unfamiliar practices, have given you a wrong impression and which you have come to know through the present confusion caused by the present, political terror. I will instead expound to you the Constitutionalism based on the Shari'a.

Constitutionalism is the manifestation of the verses, *Take counsel with them in the affairs (of public concern)* (3:159), and *Their affairs are by consultation among themselves* (42:38). This is the consultation which the Shari'a orders. The life of this luminous body is right instead of force or might. Its heart is knowledge; its tongue, love. Its reason is law, not the will of a single individual.

Constitutionalism is the rule of the people. You too will be rulers! Constitutionalism is the cause of the happiness of all peoples. You too will attain happiness! Constitutionalism awakens enthusiasm and elevated feelings. You too must awake from sleep! Constitutionalism saves humanity from bestiality. You too will be perfect humans! Constitutionalism will open the locked "good fortune" of the Muslim world and Asia. Glad tidings to you! It will be a means for our state to live forever. Our state will subsist by the subsistence of the people. Do not despair!

Constitutionalism will change the despotic, unquestionable opinion of a single individual, which, under the influence of whims and fancies, can be turned in any direction like a thin wire, into the rule of public opinion, which is like an unshakeable iron post or a shining diamond sword. You too should trust it as you trust Noah's Ark. It elevates everyone to the position of sultan; you too should try to be a sultan through the love of freedom. It secures human free will, which is the foundation of humanity, and frees humans. You too should not consent to being an inanimate object. It binds hundreds of millions of Muslims to one another like the members of a tribe. You too should preserve this bond.

The luminous representation of a Constitutionalist government is this: All of you are leaders and all of you are responsible for those whom you lead.

Force was dominant during the reign of despotism. Whoever has the sharpest sword and the hardest heart would rise. But the source, the spirit, the power, the authority, and the leadership under Constitutionalism are reason, knowledge, skills, law, and public opinion. Whoever has the sharpest reason and the most enlightened heart will rise. Since knowledge increases and strengthens, and force diminishes as they grow older, the medieval governments based on force are doomed to decline and collapse, while the contemporary governments will last, as they are founded upon knowledge.

Constitutionalism is afraid of the bears of savagery, the dragon of ignorance, and the wolves of hostility. Despair comes from impotence, and is an obstacle to every development. The spirit of struggle is firmness and steadfastness against all obstacles, however strong they are. Save yourselves from idleness. In order for Constitutionalism to come to you, lay a track of knowledge and merits so that when you board the train of perfections – civilization – and encourage the seeds of progress to board it, Constitutionalism will be able to overcome all obstacles and greet you.

The consensus of the Muslim community is a certain proof in the Shari'a. Thus, public opinion is a foundational principle of the Shari'a. The tendency of people is worthy of respect and consideration in the sight of the Shari'a.

Constitutionalism means the rule of the people. That is, the rule belongs to the parliament, which is the embodiment of public opinion. The government is only a servant. It obeys the parliament. If you have complaints about the government, you should complain about yourselves, for there is no other way to preserve your rights.

For example, if there is a change in a fountain, the water of which flows into many canals, this change will appear in all the canals. If there is a large

pool into which all the canals flow, then the pool is dependent on the fountain. Even if the pool changes completely, it will not affect the fountain.
The government is the pool and the people are the fountain. So, in order to
be able to be the fountain, we must reinforce Constitutionalism, be aware of
our rights as people, and be equipped with knowledge and merits.

(From *Münazarat* ["Discussions"])

Those who do not value Constitutionalism

QUESTION: Who are those who throw minds into confusion and do not value Constitutionalism?

ANSWER: They are a committee headed by the chieftain of ignorance,
the gentleman of obstinacy, the reverend of imitation, and the Monsieur
chatter. It is a committee that impairs consultation, which is the source of
happiness among humankind. Its members are those who do not abandon
a single lira (dollar) for a thousand liras of benefit of the nation, who find
their advantage in harming the nation, who make unbalanced and unrea-
sonable interpretations and judgments, who claim to sacrifice themselves
for the nation although they always act out of vindictiveness and personal
interest and grudges, and whose claim to support autonomy or federation is
in fact a first step toward a separate state or principality; they are those
whose claim to support a republic is actually a means to establish an absolute despotism, who wish to compensate the little wrong they suffered with
punishment and suffering for all people, and who cannot reconcile their
own vindictiveness with the freedom and ease of people.

(From *Münazarat* ["Discussions"])

A faultless government is impossible

QUESTION: How can good cause evil?

ANSWER: Demanding what is impossible is to do oneself evil. One who
takes off from a mountain in order to fly is smashed into pieces. People
wish for an innocent, faultless government. But it is not possible even for
an individual to remain or become faultless at this time. How, therefore,
can a government, especially if its parts are composed of sins, become
faultless? So we should consider whether the good of the government out-

weighs its evils. It is impossible for there to be a faultless government. I deem people who wish for an innocent government to be anarchists. For if – God forbid! – one of them were to live a thousand years and see every form of government, they would not be satisfied. They would try to destroy any form with the inclination to destruction that arises from their fancy.

(From *Münaẓarat* ["Discussions"])

The true meaning of freedom

QUESTION: Some say that freedom means that whatever one does, good or evil, cannot be questioned unless it harms others. Is this so?

ANSWER: Such claims are the ravings of those who, like children, seek pretexts for their vices; it is not freedom. True, refined freedom is taught by the Shari‘a and adorned by it with good manners. The freedom of vice and dissipation is not freedom; it is bestiality, the domination of Satan, and slavery to the carnal, evil-commanding soul.

The freedom of the people is the result of the freedom of individuals. The basic characteristic of freedom is to give no harm to both oneself and others. The perfection of freedom lies in not oppressing anyone and not mocking the freedom of others. No one should dominate others, except through the justice of law. The rights of everyone should be under protection and everyone should be free to perform lawful acts. The Divine principle, *None of us should take others for lords, apart from God* (3:64) should be the basic norm. Human freedom requires and is perfected by servanthood to God. Freedom is an attribute of belief. For the dignity of belief and the valor it gives do not allow a believer, who has become a servant of God through the bond of belief, to lower themselves before anybody else or to be under the dominion and oppression of others. Nor does the compassion which belief inculcates permit them to transgress the freedom and rights of others. The more perfect the belief, the brighter the freedom.

QUESTION: How can we be free before a great man, a saint, a great scholar? They have a right to dominate us due to their merits. We are slaves to their virtues.

ANSWER: The characteristics of sainthood and greatness are humility or modesty. They are not arrogance and domination. One who feels arrogant is one who feigns sainthood or feigns being a spiritual guide. Do not treat this person as a great one.

QUESTION: You are very hopeful about freedom and Constitutionalism. But what about the terrible snakes around us that have opened their mouths to poison our life and break our state to pieces?

ANSWER: Do not be afraid! As civilization, virtues, and freedom have begun to weigh heavier in the human realm, the other pan of the scales will gradually become lighter. Supposing the impossible – if, God forbid, they smash and kill us – for sure, we will die numbering twenty, but we will be revived numbering three hundred. Removing the dust of vices and disagreements from our heads, we will lead the caravan of humanity as a truly enlightened and united people. We do not fear such a death, which will result in the most resistant, powerful, and eternal life. Even if we die, Islam will survive. Whatever is in the future is close.

(From *Münazarat* ["Discussions"])

Can there be equality between Muslims and non-Muslims?

QUESTION: How will all be equal, including the non-Muslims among us?

ANSWER: Equality is in law, not in virtue or honor. In the sight of law, a king and a slave are the same. How can the Shari'a, which forbids treading on an ant, neglect the rights of human beings? This is not possible! But we have not been able to obey it perfectly.

The court trial of the fourth Caliph 'Ali's with an ordinary Jew, while the former was caliph, and that of Salahaddin al-Ayyubi's[62] with a Christian will correct your mistake in this matter.

Victory at the present is possible through reason, positive nationalism, progress, and justice. If one uses a sword to defeat others, their orphans (children or grandchildren) will be the target of the same sword. At the present,

---

[62] Salahaddin al-Ayyubi (1138–1193). He was one of the Sultans of the al-Ayyubis and most renowned statesmen and commanders in history. He ruled over Egypt, Syria, Iraq, Hejaz, and Yemen. He led Islamic opposition to the Franks and other European Crusaders in the Levant, and eventually recaptured Palestine from the Kingdom of Jerusalem. Salahaddin's chivalrous behavior was noted by Christian chroniclers, and despite being the nemesis of the Crusaders, he won the respect of many of them; rather than becoming a hated figure in Europe, he became a celebrated example of the principles of chivalry. (Tr.)

the sword is in the hand of reason. Our real enemies, who are destroying us, are the chieftain of ignorance, his son the gentleman of neediness, and his grandson Sir hostility. If the Armenians have treated us as enemies, they have done so under the command of these three corrupters.

(From *Münazarat* ["Discussions"])

Does the Qur'an forbid loving Christians and Jews?

QUESTION: The Qur'an forbids loving Christians and Jews: *Take not the Jews and Christians for friends and allies* (5:51). How can we make friends with them?

ANSWER: In order for a statement of the Qur'an and the Messenger to be the source of a definite, specific judgment, its meaning and purpose must be indisputably clear. This Qur'anic statement is open to interpretation and needs explanation. For the purpose and target of the prohibition it contains are not specified. So it needs to be specified. Time is a great interpreter; if it reveals restriction and specification, this should not be opposed. Furthermore, if the judgment is based on the target of the order or prohibition, this target becomes the reason for the judgment. That is, the verse forbids friendship and alliance with the Jews and Christians. This means that we cannot make friends with them in their Judaism and Christianity and act with them against believers. Moreover, a person is not loved because of themselves; they are loved because of their attributes or character and skills. Therefore, just as every attribute of a Muslim cannot be Muslim, so too, every attribute of an unbeliever does not have to originate from their unbelief. So, why should it not be permissible to appreciate or adopt a Muslim attribute and skill that is found in an unbeliever? If you have a Jewish or Christian wife, you will certainly love her because she is your wife.

Secondly, a supreme religious revolution took place during the Age of Happiness – the time of the Prophet, upon him be peace and blessings. As it turned all minds to the Religion, concentrating them on Islam, all love and enmity were purely for the sake of Religion. For this reason, any trace of love for non-Muslims gave off the smell of hypocrisy. However, since the present revolution is world-wide and takes place in the field of civilization, all minds are preoccupied with civilization, progress, and the world. Therefore, our friendship with non-Muslims is for the transference of their progress and beauty of civilization, and the preservation of public security, which is one of the foundations of worldly happiness. So, this sort of friendship is not included in the prohibition in the verse.

(From *Münazarat* ["Discussions"])

Should the Christians not be addressed as unbelievers?

QUESTION: Why should we not address the Christians as unbelievers?

ANSWER: We are not obliged to address a blind man as "O blind man!" This would be offensive. Prophetic *hadiths* prohibit offending non-Muslim citizens of a Muslim country.[63]

Secondly, the concept of unbeliever has two meanings, one of which is denier of God. We cannot attribute this meaning to the Christians. The other is denier of our Prophet and Islam. This meaning is attributable to them, and they are not offended by this attribution. However, since the concept implies the first meaning, however we use it, it has become an address of offense and insult.

Furthermore, we are not obliged to mix the sphere of belief with the sphere of mutual relations and interaction.

(From *Münazarat* ["Discussions"])

Positive and negative nationalism

We have made you into tribes and families so that you may know one another (49:13). In other words, so that you may know one another and therefore help and love one another, not so that you may remain strange to one another and be enemies to and transgressors against one another.

Just as a private soldier has a specific duty and bond in relation to the squad, platoon, and the entire hierarchy of an army, so everyone has a chain of bonds and duties in society. If these bonds and duties were not named and specified, mutual acquaintance and assistance would not emerge.

The awakening of nationalism is either positive – it revives and develops through human compassion and concern that comes from fellow-citi-

---

63   al-Munawi, *Faydu'l-Qadir*, 6:19.

zenship, which in turn leads to mutual knowing and assistance – or it is negative and rises through racist passions and tendencies, which causes mutual rejection, resistance, and enmity. Islam categorically rejects this negative nationalism.

(From *Sünuhat* ["Occurrences to the Heart"])

Response to the propaganda of unjust infidels

QUESTION: How should we respond to the propaganda of unjust infidels?

ANSWER: Propaganda is the illicit child of demagogy, which I have condemned before. Response to it should not be with a like weapon; we should respond to it with truth and honesty. A grain of truth burns away a heap of lies.

> Say "God," and then leave them to their game of plunging into vanities (6:91).

The best, cleverest trick is to abandon trickery.

(From *Tulu'at* ["Flashes of Thoughts Rising in the Heart"])

No Muslim would abandon Islam through sound reasoning

No period of history, from the Age of Happiness until now, tells us that a Muslim has preferred another religion over Islam with their sound reasoning or entered that religion based on sound proof. It is true that there have been some who have left Islam; but this has been through imitation and is of no importance. However, the followers of other religions have continuously entered the fold of Islam in throngs based on sound proof and through sound reasoning. If we demonstrate true Islam and the truth and uprightness that befit Islam, people will continue to enter it in greater numbers.

History also shows us that the development and civilization of Muslims is proportionate to their adherence to the truth of Islam, while the development and civilization of others is inversely proportionate to their religion. Also, the truth informs us that the awakening of humankind cannot be without religion. Particularly, a person who has awakened to the truth, who has come to know true humanity, and has become a candidate for the future and eternity, cannot be so without religion. For the awakening of humankind cannot occur unless it obtains the point – the nucleus of truth, i.e., the true religion – on which it will rely against the onslaughts from the universe and from which it will seek help in order to blossom its infinite ambitions and aspirations. It is because of this reality that an inclination has awakened in everyone to search for the true religion. This gives the glad tiding that humanity will naturally adopt Islam in the future.

O unfair ones! How and why do you find Islam, which has the capacity to embrace, unite, nurture, and enlighten the entire world, so narrow that you have assigned it to the poor and certain bigoted *hojas*, excluding half of its followers? Why and how do you dare imagine that the light-filled palace of Islam, which has all perfections and contains the material that will nourish the elevated feelings of all of humankind, belongs exclusively to some poor people, Bedouins, and reactionaries, as if it were a mournful, black tent? It is a fact that everyone sees and follows whatever is reflected in their mirror. This means that your dark and lying mirror shows it to be like that.

(From *Münazarat* ["Discussions"])

A Qur'anic principle of absolute justice and human capacity for great wrongdoing

> Every soul earns only to its own account; and no soul, as bearer of burden, bears and is made to bear the burden of another (6:164).

This is a most just Qur'anic principle in personal, communal, and national politics and ways of action. However:

> Man is indeed prone to doing great wrong and misjudging, and acting out of sheer ignorance (33:72).

The source of human capacity to do terrible wrong and injustice is this: unlike animals, humans are not restricted in creation in respect of their innate powers or inclinations. For this reason, unless they are guided and trained to do so, human beings do not encounter any limits to wrongdoing or egotism. When egotism, self-centeredness, selfishness, arrogance, and obstinacy are added to the human inclination to wrongdoing, humans invent such monstrous offenses and sins that they have not yet been able to name them all. As these are proofs for the necessity of Hell, their punishment can only be Hell. Consider the following:

A human being has numerous attributes or characteristics. If one of these attracts enmity, the first verse cited above requires that enmity should be restricted to only this characteristic or attribute. Having many other good attributes, that human being should only be pitied and not be a target of injustice or transgression.

However, out of untrained inclination toward wrongdoing and acting out of sheer ignorance, human beings extend enmity to all the attributes of that human being and indeed their very person. Not being content with this, they nurture enmity toward their relatives and even colleagues. However, since something may be the result of many reasons, the sinful or wrongdoing attribute deserving enmity may result from an external factor, not from the corruption of the heart. Therefore, even if this attribute is wrongful, or disbelieving, that person cannot be considered a wrongdoer.

Under the influence of vindictiveness or vindictive hostility, a greedy one forecast: "This Muslim state will disintegrate." Just to see their ominous forecast realized and so gratify their egotism and arrogance, they desire the wretchedness of Muslims and the destruction of Islamic brotherhood and unity. They want to show the monstrous injustices of the enemy as justice through demagogic arguments.

We see that the present, modern civilization has given humankind such an unjust, pitiless principle that it reduces all its virtues to nothing, and explains the reason for the concern of the angels: "*Will you set therein one who will cause disorder and corruption on it and shed blood?*" (2:30)[64]

For example, this civilization permits the destruction of a village with all the innocents in it if a traitor has taken refuge there, or the annihilation of a whole community with all its innocents, children, women, and the elderly, if one rebel is among them, or the devastation of a sacred

---

[64] Said Nursi refers to the verse of the Qur'an 2:30: Remember (when) your Lord said to the angels: "I am setting on the earth a vicegerent." The angels asked: "Will you set therein one who will cause disorder and corruption on it and shed blood, while we glorify You with Your praise (proclaiming that You are absolutely free from any defect and that all praise belongs to You exclusively,) and declare that You alone are all-holy and to be worshipped as God and Lord?" He said: "Surely I know what you do not know." Also see the following verses 31–33. (Tr.)

building of immeasurable worth, such as Ayasofya (Hagia Sofia), if one who does not obey the wrongful laws of this society seeks refuge there.

If a person is not accountable in the view of the Ultimate Truth for the sin of their brother, how can it be that thousands of innocent people are treated as responsible for the rebellion of one unruly person in a place where there may always be ill-disposed revolutionaries?

(From *Sünuhat* ["Occurrences to the Heart"])

The absolute dominion of the Qur'an Books on Islam must be binoculars through which we examine the Qur'an

Hold fast all together to the rope of God, and never be divided (6:103).

Alif-Lam-Mim. This is the Book, there is no doubt in and about it; a perfect guidance for the God-revering, pious (2:1–2).

In my judgment, the most important reason for the negligence and carelessness of the Muslim community in the observation of Islamic commands is as follows:

The pillars of the Religion and the essential, explicit commands, which form ninety percent of the Religion, belong to the Qur'an and to the Sunna, which interprets the Qur'an. The controversial matters which are referred to the legal procedures of the scholars who are qualified to exercise *ijtihad* constitute only the remaining ten percent. There is a great difference in value between the pillars and essential commands of the Religion and its controversial matters which are referred to the discretion of the scholars. If the latter are gold, the former are diamonds. Is it reasonable or religiously permissible to leave ninety diamond pillars to the protection of ten pieces of gold?

Rather than rational and religious arguments, the sacredness of the source of the Religion urges the common people to observe it. The books of the eminent scholars should be like glass – they should display the Qur'an, not overshadow it.

It has been logically established that the mind moves from something necessary to that which makes it necessary, or its conditioning precedent. It does not naturally move from a conditioning precedent to that which is the source of this precedent. Even if it does move in that direction, it does so with a new intention and attention. This is not natural.

For example, the books on the Shari'a from which we learn the commands of the Shari'a are necessary (to study and follow). The Qur'an, which is their basic source, is what makes them necessary to follow. The sacredness of the Qur'an and its Author, which moves human conscience, is the primary, basic motive for the observation of the commands of the Shari'a. However, since the views of common people are concentrated on the books of the Shari'a, they only maintain a vague view of the Qur'an. They rarely give the sacredness of the Qur'an and its Author the attention due. It is because of this that conscience is accustomed to a solidified indifference.

If attention had been made to concentrate on the Qur'an itself in the books on the essentials and basic commands of the Religion, minds would automatically have turned to the sacredness of the Source – the Revealer – of the Qur'an, which encourages adherence to Him, and awakens conscience, and which is an essential aspect of it. This would also have caused the heart to develop sensitivity and have prevented it from remaining deaf to the warnings and encouragements of belief.

This means that, while the books on the Shari'a should have been like pieces of glass through which the Qur'an could be read, over time, they have rusted due to the errors of imitative and quoting writers, and veiled the Qur'an. The books which should have been exponents of the Qur'an are rather separate, independent works.

The Qur'an is the eternal Divine Address and is always new and fresh due to its miraculousness and it is hallowed by its All-Sacred Origin; it always moves the conscience through belief. There are three ways to attract the attention of the common people to it:

- Destroying through criticism the renown, respect, and trustworthiness which the authors of the books on Shari'a have deservedly gained. This is dangerous, unfair, and unjust.
- Transforming the books on the Shari'a through gradual, particular education into transparent exponents of the Qur'an, through which the Qur'an can be seen and read. The books written by the *mujtahids* among the early generations of Islam, such as *al-Muwat-*

ta' by Imam Malik,[65] and *al-Fiqhu'l-Akbar*, written by Imam Abu Hanifa[66] are of this kind.

For example, when a person applies to Ibn Hajar,[67] they should apply to him in order to understand the Qur'an and learn what it says, not in order to understand what Ibn Hajar says. This second way requires time.

- In the same way that some great guides of the Islamic spiritual way have done, the attention of the common people should be drawn from the veils of the Qur'an to the Qur'an itself and the pure property of the Qur'an should be requested from the Qur'an itself; secondary commands deduced by the *mujtahids* should be sought from the *mujtahids* themselves or from the relevant books. It is due to this that the sermons of spiritual guides are usually more attractive and effective than those of the scholars of the Shari'a.

It is a social fact that the reward, demand, and attention which public esteem assigns to something is not due to its essential value, but to the common people's need for it. A watchmaker's earning more than a great scholar proves this. If, therefore, the essential religious needs of the Muslim community had been directed toward the Qur'an, if Muslim peoples had understood that they needed the Qur'an more than anything else and sought the satisfaction of their needs in the Qur'an, that Book, clear in itself and clearly showing the truth, would have been much more in demand than the demand distributed among millions of other books, and as a result of such a need the Qur'an would have received much more attention. Thus, it would have been absolutely dominant and influential among people. It would not have remained as a blessed book whose blessing is sought merely in the recitation of it.

---

[65]   Imam Malik ibn Anas (711–795): He has born, lived, and died in Madina. He was one of the most highly respected scholars of *fiqh* (Islamic jurisprudence) and the Maliki School of Law was named after him. (Tr.)

[66]   Imam A'zam Abu Hanifa, Nu'man ibn Thabit (d. 768): He founded the Hanafi School of Law and was one of the greatest Muslim scholars of jurisprudence and deducer of new laws from the Qur'an and Sunnah. He also was well-versed in theology. (Tr.)

[67]   Al-Hafiz Shihabuddin Abu'l-Fadl Ahmad ibn Ali, known as Ibn Hajari'l-Asqalani, 1372–1448) was a medieval Shafi'i Sunni scholar of Islam. He was one of the greatest scholars of Hadith and also a renowned expert in Shafi'i jurisprudence. Ibn Hajar authored more than fifty works on Hadith, Hadith terminology, history, biography, Qur'anic interpretation, poetry and Shafi'i jurisprudence. (Tr.)

It is another great fault to combine the essentials and basic commands of the Religion with secondary, controversial matters of the Shari'a and to make the former dependent on the latter. There are two approaches to the differences of view on those secondary matters. The first is *Musawwiba*, which holds that there can be more than one truth concerning secondary, controversial matters, and therefore all of the four basic schools of law are true in their conclusions. The other is *Mukhattia*, the school which claims that all of the schools may be wrong in their conclusions. The *Musawwiba* says: "I maintain that our way is correct, but it is possible that it is wrong. Other ways are wrong, but it is equally possible that they are correct." The common people cannot distinguish between the basic, explicit commands of the Religion, which are also included in the conclusions of the schools of law, and the secondary, controversial matters, all of which they may consider – the basic, explicit commands and the schools of law's judgments concerning the secondary matters – as possibly wrong. This is an extremely grave and dangerous error. Those who maintain that all the schools of law may be wrong in their conclusions concerning the secondary, controversial matters are suffering from the disease of holding a monopoly on thinking and truths, which arises from self-love. They are also responsible for heedlessness to the comprehensiveness of the Qur'an and its accessibility to all levels of understanding of all classes of people at all times.

Since the approach of the *Mukhattia* is also the origin of suspicion, ill-opinion of others, and partiality, it has caused great injury to the solidarity of spirits, unity of hearts, and mutual love and assistance, which are essential to Islam and the life of Muslims – indeed, we are commanded to hold a good opinion of one another, to love one another, and to be united.

(From *Sünuhat* ["Occurrences to the Heart"])

What should be done for the desired future of the Kurds and Turks?

QUESTION: What do you suggest be done for the development and desired future of the Kurds and Turks?

ANSWER: I suggest that a university, to be called *Medresetu'z-Zehra*, should be opened in Bitlis, which is the center of the region of Kurds, and in Van and Diyarbakır, two wings of Bitlis. Be sure that we Kurds do not resemble others; we certainly know that our social life depends on the life and happiness of the Turks.

QUESTION: How? In what way? Why?

ANSWER: This suggestion has certain prerequisites and fruits.

QUESTION: What are its prerequisites?

ANSWER: There are eight.

The first is that the name *medrese* is known and pleasing to everybody, and is attractive and arouses zeal. It also contains a great truth and therefore stirs up the demand for education.

The *second* is that the positive sciences should be studied together with the religious sciences, and Arabic should be obligatory, Turkish compulsory, and Kurdish permissible.

QUESTION: What wisdom is there in studying these two kinds of sciences that you support it so whole-heartedly and always suggest it?

ANSWER: Such study will save the intellectual reasoning from the darkness of the fallacies that result from four corrupted analogies or comparisons[68] and remove the sophistry to which philosophical approaches have given rise in parasitic imitators.

QUESTION: In what way?

ANSWER: The light of conscience is religious sciences, and the light of reason or intellect is physical sciences. The truth is manifested from their fusion. The endeavor of students soars on these two wings. When they remain separate, the religious sciences cause bigotry, while the physical sciences give rise to doubt and deception.

The third prerequisite is appointing teachers among the Kurdish scholars who know the regional language and whom both the Turks and Kurds trust, scholars who are well-versed in both religious knowledge and spirituality.

---

[68] These four analogies or comparisons are (1) comparing the material or physical with the spiritual and accepting the modern, European view and position as the norm in spiritual matters, and accepting the views of some famous people in a field of science as proof in other sciences as well; (2) rejecting the view of religious scholars who have no knowledge of physical sciences in religious sciences; (3) trusting in oneself in religious matters out of arrogance resulting from their knowledge of physical sciences; (4) comparing earlier generations with new ones and the past with the present, and raising wrongful objections to the Religion. (Abdulmecid Ünlükul, the brother of Said Nursi)

The fourth is consulting the capacity of Kurds and considering their simplicity and infancy in sciences. For garments are of different sizes according to the size of a people; a garment fit for one size is ugly for another. The education of children is based on either compulsion or flattering their fancies and desires.

The fifth is completely complying with the principle of the division of labor so that, although the branches of science cannot utterly be separated from one another and are interconnected, specialists may be brought up in every branch.

The sixth is finding a source of nourishment for the students and establishing this university as an equal to other universities in every official respect.

The seventh is that until this university is built, the School of Teachers should be given a central position in Istanbul University and reorganized from the same perspective, so that it may be reflected or imitated in this new one, and the virtues and religiousness of this one may be transmitted to the other. Thus both may have two wings (one scientific thought and approach and the other, religiousness and spirituality).

The eighth is that individual education, which is the usual way in the Kurdish region, should be replaced by collective education.

QUESTION: What are the benefits?

ANSWER: Islamic and patriotic zeal and endeavor.

QUESTION: What else?

ANSWER: This *medrese* contains, like a seed, the tree of *Touba*.[69] If it grows and blossoms through zeal and endeavor, it will come to the point of meeting its expenses by itself, growing independent of your nearly-empty purses.

QUESTION: How?

ANSWER: *The first* is that if the pious foundations are well organized, they will allow a significant amount of "water" to flow to this pool through the canal of the unification of *medreses*.

The second is the *Zakah* (the Prescribed Purifying Alms). After a while, that *Medresetu'z-Zehra* will deservedly assign to itself some of the *Zakah*

---

[69]   The tree of *Touba* is the tree of Paradise and symbolizes being huge with numerous branches. (Tr.)

through the service it provides to Islam and humanity. Even the *zakah* of the *Zakah* will be sufficient.

The third is that in addition to this *medrese* being the highest school of sciences in the sight of intellects through the fruit it will yield, the light it will scatter, and the service it will do for Islam, it will also be the perfect religious school (*medrese*) in the view of hearts, and the most sacred dervish lodge in the view of consciences. Since it will be both a school, a *medrese*, and a dervish lodge at the same time, the charities and the payments to be made for the fulfillment of vows, which are the "national" donations of Islam, will flow into it.

The fourth is that since its task will be fulfilled by the School of Teachers for a limited period of time, the income of this school will increase, and the surplus will be directed to *Medresetu'z-Zehra* as a loan. After some time, the *medrese* will become independent and repay its loan.

QUESTION: What further expectations do you have from this *medrese*, about which you have clamoring for over ten years?

ANSWER: To summarize my further expectations – it will secure the future of Kurdish scholars, introduce scientific knowledge to the region of the Kurds, and demonstrate the beauties of Constitutionalism and freedom so that people may benefit from them.

QUESTION: This is worth further explanation.

ANSWER: *Firstly*: The *medreses* will be united and reformed.

Secondly: Islam will be saved from unsubstantiated narratives, Israelite stories and information, and cold bigotry. The character of Islam is a religious firmness formed of steadfastness, commitment, determination, and the support of right and truth. It is not bigotry arising from ignorance or the lack of reasoning. In my opinion, the most formidable and incurable bigotry or fanaticism is found in the blind imitators of Europe. They obstinately insist on their superficial doubts. This is not the attitude of religious scholars who act on proof.

Thirdly: A door will be opened to spread the beauties of Constitutionalism. The Kurds have no intention of harming Constitutionalism, but if it is not appreciated well, this may also lead to harm. If a patient supposes a cure to be mixed with poison, they will certainly not use it.

Fourthly: A way will be opened for a new style of education to enter *medreses* and a pure source of sciences acceptable to the people of *medreses* will be formed. For I have repeatedly said that an evil understanding and image have prevented the realization of these.

Fifthly: I have repeated nearly one hundred times, but I will repeat again: the people or members of the *medreses* (purely religious schools) and (secular) schools and spiritual centers should be reconciled. They should at least agree on their main purpose through the exchange of inclinations and opinions. Do we not witness, regrettably, that their disparity in views has caused disunity and their varying ways have prevented progress? Each group goes to extremes because they show fanatical adherence to their own way and because they have superficial knowledge of other ways. While one group sees the other as being misguided, the other accuses the former of ignorance.

In short: If Islam takes on a physical form, it will be manifested as a lofty, light-filled and well-built palace; one of the rooms of this palace will be the school of sciences, another, the *medrese*, or the school of religious sciences, and still another, the dervish lodge; its hall will be the meeting salon of all who gather together as a consultative committee to complete each other's shortcomings. Just as a mirror represents the sun according to its capacity, so too will the *Medresetu'z-Zehra* represent that Divine palace in the physical realm.

(From *Münazarat* ["Discussions"])

How can Muslims recover and preserve their honor?

QUESTION: How can we gather our power and preserve our national (Islamic) honor?

ANSWER: Make a large pool of knowledge, skills, and love in the bosom of the nation with Islamic nationalism. Plug the leaks and holes at the bottom with education. Open canals to let water flow into it with Islamic virtues. There is a great fountain; its water has so far been directed to deserts, and has fed some beggars and impotent ones. Build a beautiful canal from this fountain, and fill this with the produce of your work in accordance with the Shari'a, and allow the water to flow into the pool. Water your garden of perfections with it. This is an inexhaustible source.

QUESTION: What is that fountain?

ANSWER: It is the *Zakah*. You have intelligence; it will blossom through the *Zakah*.

QUESTION: How?

ANSWER: If the intelligent spend the *zakah* of their intelligence, and the rich spend the *zakah* of their wealth on the interests of the nation, our nation will catch up with other nations.

QUESTION: What else?

ANSWER: The payments made in the fulfillment of promises or vows and charities are the cousins of *Zakah*; they will help with this service.

QUESTION: Why do you disparage many of our established customs?

ANSWER: There is a rule for every age. This age sentences certain old customs to death. As their harm is greater than their benefit, they should be executed.

QUESTION: What is most necessary for us?

ANSWER: Truthfulness.

QUESTION: What else?

ANSWER: Not to tell lies.

QUESTION: And then?

ANSWER: Trustworthiness, sincerity, faithfulness, steadfastness, and solidarity.

QUESTION: Only these?

ANSWER: Yes.

QUESTION: Why?

ANSWER: Unbelief is a lie, while belief is truth. Is this not proof enough that our survival is possible through belief, truthfulness, and solidarity?

(From *Münazarat* ["Discussions"])

The present condition of medreses and religious scholars

QUESTION: The religious scholars have been much disparaged ...?

ANSWER: If a scholar does not have the mildness required by learning, condemning knowledge due to the faults that arise from a lack of mildness in a scholar is idiocy. So, if it is not idiocy, what is it then to condemn the scholars who always, according to their capacities, inculcate the sacredness of Islam, communicate the decrees or the commands of Islam, and now deserve the greatest respect, love, and compassion among Muslim people because there are no scholars of the same caliber at the present time?

We have suffered no harm because of the existence of religious scholars, but we have suffered harm due to a lack of scholars we need. At the present time, those of high intelligence have preferred the schools of sciences; the wealthy ones have not consented to the livelihood of the *medreses*. Since the *medreses* have been left deprived of the necessary organization, the required standard of learning, and an outlet in the modern world, they have not been able to raise the scholars that are needed by our time. Never dislike the scholars; disliking them is a great fault and dangerous.

(From *Münazarat* ["Discussions"])

On differences and disagreements among the scholars of the Muslim world

QUESTION: What is your view of the great differences and disagreements among the scholars of the Muslim world?

ANSWER: I view the world of Islam as a parliament or consultative assembly which has fallen out of order. The Shari'a pronounces that the opinion of the majority is acceptable and judgment is based on it. Other opinions can be left to the choice of different individual capacities, provided they are not altogether devoid of truth or an acceptable essence, as befits their education. However, the following two points are worthy of note:

The first is that although an opinion which has only a certain degree of truth in it and is unacceptable to the majority should remain restricted and particular to the capacity which adopts it, its owner leaves it to roam free. Others who adopt and generalize it, and its imitators, hold fast to it so fanatically that in order to preserve it they try to refute and destroy its opponents. This gives rise to such competition, mutual refutation, and condemnation that the dust rising from under the feet, the smoke coming out of the mouths, and the thunderstorm breaking out on the tongues make up a dark cloud before the sun of Islam. Not only can this cloud not hold or yield merciful rain, it also blocks out the light of the sun.

The second point is that if the truth contained in an opinion that is adopted by only a few cannot overcome the personal disposition, desires, and fancies of those who prefer it, it becomes dangerous. For while the capacities adopting it should assume its color and act according to its imperative, they in fact adapt it to suit their own personal disposition and fancies, and subjugate it to themselves. This leads guidance to be transformed into fancy and whim and the way is nourished by personal disposition. An insect drinks a fluid and produces honey, while a snake drinks water and produces poison.

However, it is my certain hope that on this ecstatically revolving earth a high assembly of Muslim scholars will constitute a sacred parliament of knowledge. The predecessors (those who came earlier) and the successors (those to come later) will look at each other over centuries and between them give rise to a consultative assembly.

Secondly, as another cause of harmful disagreement, the statements: "Only this is the truth" instead of "This is true," and "Only this is beautiful" instead of "This is beautiful" have been adopted. "Hatred for God's sake" has been substituted for "loving for God's sake." Instead of loving one's way, hatred for other ways has directed manners and behaviors. Self-centeredness has replaced the love of truth. Means, vehicles, and arguments have been taken for the goals, destinations, and ends.

However, it may sometimes occur that a wrong, false means or argument may help to reach a true goal or a true result. When the purpose and goal are true, defect and corruption in the means and arguments should not cause discord or division of hearts.

Thirdly, demagogy, which is oppressive, is another cause of disagreement among religious scholars. Demagogy or loquaciousness, which arises from criticism and pessimism, is always wrongful and oppressive.

QUESTION: What do you mean by demagogy or loquaciousness?

ANSWER: Seeing only the faults and defects in varied, vast affairs is demagogy; it is both deceived and deceiving. The essence of demagogy is exaggerating an evil to the extent that it veils good.

The entire universe is weeping in great sorrow at the sight of a mother who feels excessive grief over the death of her child. Do wisdom and usefulness in existence agree with such an impression, one that weighs down the delight in human life with grief?

A tired traveler enters a very beautiful, well-laid out garden for an hour's rest, and then notices – according to the principle that only the gardens of Paradise can be free of all filth and defect and that there is defect in every perfection in this world of formation and deformation – some filthy things in different corners of the garden. On account of his own evil disposition, he sees only those things, perceiving the garden as if it were entirely full of filth, and this negative impression may be so enlarged by his imagination as to convince him that the entire garden is a filthy and foul place. As a result, his stomach becomes upset, he vomits, and flees from the garden in utter disgust.

One who sees the good side of everything thinks good. One who thinks of good enjoys life.

QUESTION: How can the differences and disagreements in the Muslim world be eliminated?

ANSWER: First of all, we should concentrate on the basic points of agreement. Our God is one, our Prophet is one, our Qur'an is one, and we are all agreed on the essentials of the Religion. Disagreement on the secondary matters and detail cannot and must not shake this unity. Secondly, if "loving for God's sake" is adopted as a principle and love of truth directs our attitudes and behavior – time and conditions help us greatly with these matters – our differences and disagreement can be directed into accurate, straight channels.

Regrettably, if the main objective is forgotten or neglected, the minds turn to individual egos and revolve around them.

The various parts of an institution should be in harmony with one another. Personal merits and capabilities should not give way to disagreement and discord. Individual egos should be torn apart and "we" should emerge.

(From *Tulu'at* ["Flashes of Thoughts Rising in the Heart"])

Different types of leaders, chieftains, religious scholars, and guides

QUESTION: There are two kinds of leaders, chieftains, religious scholars, and guides. What are the differences between them?

ANSWER: If a "great" man relies on force, intrigue, and the spiritual power which he feigns to have, even though he does not have it, and treats people as if they were slaves or servants – if he reduces humanity to the level of animals through the pressure of fear and compulsion, and always causes people to lose their eagerness, zeal, and joy, then he is a despotic leader, chieftain, or religious guide. If there is a success or victory, it is attributed only to that despotic one, but if there is evil or a defeat, it is divided among his poor subjects. Such a "great" one is not great; in truth, he is small. He humiliates and underrates his people. People do whatever they must reluctantly and only for the sake of that man. Even if they do good, they do it hypocritically, and thus are accustomed to sycophancy and lying. They are constantly in decline, since enthusiasm, which is the steam power of human endeavor, has been extinguished. Their leaders and chieftains sit on their shoulders so that only they may be seen. They eat of their flesh so that they may grow. Such leaders curtain the rosebud-like capacities of the people and shut off the light so that only they themselves may grow and blossom.

However, a truly great man relies on right and truth, uses intellect, binds his people to himself through love, and instead of getting on the shoulders of their successes, he gets under them and awakens their enthusiasm. If there is good, he divides it among his people; by giving everyone a part of it, he increases their zeal. He sets his people against the light of knowledge so that right and justice may prevail. He sends the water of love and intellect to the rosebud-like capacities and feelings of the people so that they may develop and blossom. Such a leader is the concrete example of the Prophetic definition of leader: "The leader of a people is he who serves them."[70]

(From Münazarat ["Discussions"])

Awakening spiritual guides

QUESTION: Why do you attack the spiritual guides of the time? There are saints among them. Do you not fear that you attack them ignorantly and are you not regretful about what you have done?

---

[70]   al-Ajluni, Kashfu'l-Khafa', 2:463.

ANSWER: God the Almighty, Exalted is His Majesty, inscribed the truth on their elevated forehead with His Power. My purpose is to awaken those who are thirsty for this inscription of truth.

They cannot prevent me from my way with threats. I am determined to take every risk on my way to my goal. While an ordinary non-Muslim sacrifices their life for their nation, my bond with my life is extremely weak. My life has, to date, almost flown from my hand seven times, but it has been left in my hand. I have no right to put anyone under obligation by giving my life for the sake of my cause. Although my spirit desires to fly from its cage onto the tree, and my mind wants to flee from my head into despair, they have been left in their places so that I might sacrifice them later. So it is in vain to threaten me with death. They also threaten me with losing the afterlife. No matter! I am burning in the fire of sorrows and sighs for our present condition, and resound with regret at our neglect and loss. If I burn in Hellfire due to their malediction, my conscience will feel paradisiacal happiness at being saved from this fire of sorrows, sighs, and regrets, and my imagination will build a paradise out of hope and aspiration. Let everyone know that I am carrying my two lives – this and the next – in my two hands, and am preoccupied with fighting against two enemies at the fronts. Let no one with only one life come up against me!

QUESTION: What do you want from the present guides?

ANSWER: I want them to have sincerity or purity of intention which they always mention; I want them to exert themselves to fight against their souls – the major *jihad* – which is their duty in their military job – spiritual purification, to abandon pursuing their personal interests and to lead an austere life, which is their claim and distinguishing mark, and to love each other, which they always claim and advise, and which is the essence of an Islamic disposition. They have received their wages by employing us, now it is their duty to serve us.

QUESTION: How should they act?

ANSWER: They should either give up claiming guidance or remove obstinacy, backbiting, and bias from among themselves. Some innovative guides have caused the formation of certain schools of deviation and innovation.

QUESTION: How can they be united while some deny the others?

ANSWER: Have you not heard and understood that *"The believers are but only brothers (and sisters) (49:10)"* is a Divine principle, and do you not see that "No one among you will believe unless he desires for his brother (sister) what he desires for himself"[71] is a Prophetic principle? How could it be that denial of others is able to abrogate these two firm, essential foundations? Even if they deny each other, it is not a Divine word so that it cannot be abrogated. Moreover, since its harm surpasses its benefit, then time has abrogated it. It is not permissible to act according to a rule that is already abrogated.

QUESTION: Their mutual dislike may be due to the evils they have suffered at each other's hand.

ANSWER: How can this be? According to what justice and fairness? How could it be that the love resulting from and required by belief, by being Muslims, and by fellowship in humanity, has been overcome by the hostility caused by some petty unIslamic acts and ways of treatment, which is no more than a childish pretext? Being Muslims and being part of humanity, which require mutual love, are like Mount Uhud in weight, while the causes that give rise to hostility are like pebbles. Defeating love by hostility is so idiotic an act that it means reducing Mount Uhud to the lightness of a few pebbles. Like light and darkness, love and hostility cannot exist together. If hostility wins, love changes into flattery and hypocrisy; if love overcomes then hostility is transformed into pity and compassion. My way is loving love and being hostile to hostility. What I love most in the world is love and what I resent most is hostility.

QUESTION: What is the difference between a saintly guide and one who claims to guide?

ANSWER: If one's purpose is to combine the Islamic light of heart with the light of mind, if their way is based on love and characterized by humility or modesty, if the distinguishing mark of their way is selflessness and avoidance of pursuing personal interests, and if one acts out of Islamic zeal and for the victory of Islam – then we may hope that such a one is a true guide. However, if their way is characterized by criticizing others to show themselves as meritorious and virtuous, by trying to inculcate their love by cherishing hostility toward others, and by bias or partiality – which causes division of power, and if their love depends on hostility toward others, which gives rise to backbiting, then such a one is a seditious, misguiding claimer of guidance, and a wolf

---

[71]   al-Bukhari, "Iman" 6; Muslim, "Iman" 71.

in pursuit of plunder. They drum on the spiritual way with their hands instead of playing the drum so that they may be tipped and receive gifts. They attempt to hunt the world with the Religion. They have been deceived either by a poisonous pleasure or a lowly fancy or a wrong reasoning and deduction, thus they suppose themselves to be great and have opened the way to having an ill-opinion of truly great guides and holy persons.

(From *Münaẓarat* ["Discussions"])

Taking action for the sake of the Religion

They asked me: "You see that irreligion is spreading; is it not necessary to take action to serve the Religion?"

ANSWER: Yes, it is necessary, but provided what urges us to come forward in the name of Religion is love of Islam and religious zeal. If the motive is politics and partisanship, it is dangerous. If we err in the first case, it will be forgivable, but even if we succeed in the second case, we will be responsible for the consequences.

They asked: "How are we to understand whether the motive is politics or love of Islam?"

ANSWER: Whoever prefers their transgressing, sinful fellow-partisan to their religious political opponent due to political pretexts, their motive is politics. Also, if due to a monopoly of views one presents the Religion, to which all Muslims belong, as restricted to fellow-partisans, it will arouse opposition to the Religion in a powerful majority and cause the Religion to be disfavored. This shows that the motive is politics. One can serve the Religion by guiding people to the Religion, encouraging them to observe it, and reminding them of their religious duties. Accusing some people of irreligion means pushing them to attack the Religion. The Religion should not be used for negative motives or negative ends within a Muslim land.

(From *Sünuhat* ("Occurrences to the Heart"))

Belief and love, faithfulness, and Islamic patriotism and zeal

Those who see me during my travels think that I am a trader and ask me whether I am a trader.

ANSWER: I am a trader and chemist.

QUESTION: What do you trade in?

ANSWER: In two substances: I mix them, and one is transformed into a cure, and the other into illuminating electricity.

QUESTION: Where are they found?

ANSWER: In the marketplace of true civilization and virtues. They are contained in a brilliant black box, on which "heart" is written; this exists in the chest that stands on two legs and on whose forehead is written "man."

QUESTION: What are their names?

ANSWER: Belief and love, faithfulness, and Islamic patriotism and zeal.

(From *Münazarat* ["Discussions"])

Islamic unity

QUESTION: What do you understand by the term Islamic unity?

ANSWER: Look to the foundations or embroidery of Islamic unity: in it are fused the innocent courage and chivalry that originate from modesty and patriotic zeal, the innocent smile engendered by respect and compassion, the spiritual beauty resulting from goodness, elegance, and generosity of spirit, the heavenly joy issuing from innocent love and ever-fresh enthusiasm, the transcendental pleasure springing from lofty sorrow and sinless exhilaration, and the sacred adornment that comes from abstract beauty and brilliant grace. The luminous color resulting from this fusion represents the image of the seven colors of the rainbow of the elevated arch of the Ka'ba of happiness, in which the east and west join together.

However, such unity is not possible with ignorance; unity is the harmony of ideas, which comes about through the electric light of knowledge and education.

(From *Münazarat* ["Discussions"])

Part Four

Part Four

Miscellaneous Matters

The testimony of human conscience to God the Almighty

ONSCIENCE IS HUMAN CONSCIOUS NATURE, THE POINT OF THE inter-section between the Unseen and the visible, corporeal realms, where the tides between these two realms meet. Concerning its testimony to God the Almighty, consider the following four points:

THE FIRST: A thing's innate drive or its God-given nature does not lie. For example, a seed's urge to grow says: "I will grow into such-and-such a plant and produce fruit," and then it does so. An egg's urge to life says: "I will be a chick," and then becomes a chick. Water's urge to freeze says: "I will take up more space," and then it does so. Hard and solid iron cannot contradict it; rather, when frozen, water splits it. Such drives and urges are manifestations of the Divine commands of creation that issue from the Divine Will.

THE SECOND: Apart from their five external senses and certain other inner ones, a person also has many windows that open unto the Unseen world, and many other, imperceptible senses. We have a sixth sense of drive or urge and the seventh sense of enthusiasm. Those two senses cannot lie or mislead.

THE THIRD: An imaginary thing cannot be the origin or cause of an external fact or reality. The existence of the point of reliance and the point of seeking help in human conscience is an undeniable reality. Without it, the human spirit, which is the most refined extract and noblest of creation, would be the lowliest and most wretched creature. But the wisdom in the existence of the universe and its order and perfection refute this probability.

THE FOURTH: Even if reason abandons its essential duty and sees and judges wrongly, human conscience cannot forget its Maker. Even if it denies its own existence, the conscience thinks of Him, sees Him, and is turned to Him. Intuition, which is a power of quick, lightning-like grasp, continuously provokes it. Inspiration, which is doubled intuition, constantly illuminates it. Desire, which is doubled inclination, yearning, doubled desire, and love of God, the doubled yearning, always stimulate it toward knowledge of the All-Majestic One. The feelings of attraction and being attracted felt in one's innate human conscience are due to the attractive power of this substantial truth.

The human conscious nature, which we call conscience, and which distinguishes between what is good and evil, which feels pleasure and exhilaration in what is good, and suffers from and is grieved by what is evil, consists of four basic elements, namely the spiritual intellect, the willpower, the mind, and the power of perceptiveness. These four elements are also regarded as the senses of the spirit. In addition to their different duties and functions, each of these senses has an ultimate purpose for its existence. The ultimate purpose for willpower is worshipping God; for the mind, it is having knowledge of God, for the power of perceptiveness, it is love of God, and for the spiritual intellect it is vision of God. What we call taqwa (piety and righteousness), which is the perfect form or degree of worship, is the result of the functions of all these four senses. The Shari‘a nourishes them so that they develop, equips them with the necessary material, and directs them to the ultimate purposes for the existence of each.

(From Noqta ["The Point"])

The ways to attain knowledge of the Creator

There are four ways to attain knowledge of the Creator, which is the highest point human beings can reach:

THE FIRST is the way of the scholarly Sufis, based on the purification of the soul, refinement of the heart, and inner illumination and observation.

THE SECOND is the way of the theologians. It is based on two arguments. *The first* is that the existence of the universe is not necessary, because the universe's existence is not by itself and the universe itself has nothing of its own which can necessitate its existence; it is equally possible that it would or would not come into existence. It is contained in time and space, or is accidental or contingent. Consequently there must be One Who willed it and brought it into existence. *The second argument* is that the universe is not timeless or without beginning: it has a starting point, and this requires the existence of One unbounded by time Who brought it into existence.

Both of these ways are derived from the Qur'an, but human thought has given them their own forms and elaborated on them accordingly.

THE THIRD WAY belongs to the people of wisdom or the believing philosophers. This way is open to controversy and the assault of whims or suspicion.

THE FOURTH WAY is the way of the Qur'an, which is the most direct and clearest of ways, one which shows the peerless eloquence of the Qur'an and is possible for all to follow. There are four means to climb to this highest station: inspiration; study; the correction of wrong information, prejudices, wrong perspectives, and sins or sinful attitudes such as oppression and arrogance; and a correct viewpoint.

The way of the Qur'an is principally based on two arguments. *The first* is the argument of the perfect order of the universe and mutual assistance, beneficence and purposefulness. All of the Qur'anic verses that mention the purposes and benefits of things are indicative of this argument. This argument is based on the fact that the perfect universal order takes into account beneficence and purposefulness. Whatever exists serves many benefits and purposes and has many instances of wisdom. As a corollary of this argument, any notion of chance or coincidence in the creation of beings is categorically rejected. Perfection or faultlessness is impossible without a determining will. By showing the fruits and purposes that hang from the links of the chains of creatures, and the instances of wisdom, uses and benefits concealed in the knots of the changes and transformations of conditions and states in existence, all the sciences that study the universe and witness its perfect order bear decisive witness to the Maker's purpose and wisdom. For example:

The sciences of botany and zoology bear witness to the fact that millions of plant and animal species came into existence at a point in time and each ends in a father or mother-individual. What we call laws, whose existence we deduce from the working of the universe and who we name, and therefore which are nominal, and blind, unconscious natural causes, are absolutely devoid of any capacity – knowledge, will, and power – to originate, form, or develop these amazing chains of the beings and the individuals – those Divine machines – that form them. Therefore, each individual and each species demonstrates and announces that they have been produced by the Hand of an All-Wise Maker's Power. The Qur'an says: *Look yet again: can you see any rifts?* (67: 3)

The Qur'an expounds the argument of beneficence and purposefulness in the most perfect fashion. In addition to ordering reflection on the universe, in the conclusive parts of the verses that mention the purposes and benefits of things, the Qur'an commands and warns with such statements as *Think and take lessons! Do they not know? Do they not reason? Do they not remember and take heed?*, calling us to use our reason and consult our conscience. Thus, it establishes the argument of beneficence and purposefulness.

The second Qur'anic argument for God Almighty's Existence and Oneness is that of creation or origination. Its summary is as follows:

Every species, and each member of that species, has been given an existence that accords with the function or purpose assigned to it and the inherent capacity it possesses. In addition, no species is a link in a chain that stretches back to the eternity of the past so that it can also be the originator of the chain, for the existence of each species is contingent, not absolute. (There is a Will that makes a preference between the existence and non-existence of each thing and a Power that gives it existence. Existence is clearly not timeless, but is contained in time and space, and therefore has a beginning.) A truth or an established reality cannot become its opposite, nor can its nature change. Hybrid species – like mules – which are the offspring of two different species, cannot reproduce. They are exceptions and never mean the complete transformation of an established truth, which is impossible. What people call matter is not separate from or independent of a changeable form or the motions and changes which occur within time. Therefore, matter also has a beginning and is time-bound. Being accidental and time-bound, forces and forms cannot be the cause of the essential differentiation between species. Something accidental cannot be the original substance or essence. This means that all the links that form species and their distinguishing features originate from non-existence. The successive generation or reproduction in species is only among certain apparent, nominal conditions for their life and survival.

How strange a misguidance that those who cannot attribute to God His essential Attributes and manifestations, such as eternity and creativity, in their reason are able to ascribe them to lifeless, powerless, unconscious, and time-bound matter or atoms. How can the huge universe submit itself to the control and management of the motion of tiny atoms instead of the Hand of the Divine Eternal Power? How can origination and creation, which are particular to the Eternal Divine Power, be attributed to the poorest and most powerless causes, which have nothing to do with originating and creating?

In consequence, the Qur'an establishes this argument with its verses that mention creation and origination. The True Cause is only God. Other causes have no creative part in the existence or life of things. These causes are veils before the dignity and grandeur of the Divine Power, so that the Hand of Power will not be seen by a superficial reason as being related to mean acts and affairs.

Everything has two aspects or faces; one is corporeal, like the dark face of a mirror. Opposites, such as ugliness and beauty, evil and good, small and large, occur in this face. A role has been assigned to causes in this face, as the manifestation of Divine Grandeur and the dignity of the Power require it to be so.

The other is the transparent, immaterial aspect or face, like the transparent face of a mirror. Everything is pure and beautiful in this face and causes have no part or effect at all. Divine Unity requires this to be so. It is for this reason that, as both faces of life, spirit – which is the light of life – and existence are pure, transparent and beautiful, causes have no part in either of their faces and they are directly created by the Hand of Divine Power.

Things such as gravity, motion, and force are in fact the names of God's habitual acts in the universe. Provided they are not taken for real causes or forces that are responsible for the occurrences in the universe, they may be called laws.

(From *Noqta* ["The Point"])

Polygamy and slavery in the sight of the Shari'a

QUESTION: Foreigners cast doubt on the Shari'a from the viewpoint of civilization on certain pretexts such as polygamy and slavery.

ANSWER: I will express a principle for the time being; I am contemplating explaining such matters in a separate booklet.

Islam has two sorts of legal codes. One is that on which the Shari'a is based; all the principles and commands included in this code are pure good and beauty.

The second is that the Shari'a has balanced and improved the code. That is, the Shari'a saved the principles and laws included in this code from being cruel and oppressive; it has amended them and put them in a practicable form suited to the essential human nature, and entrusted them to time so that they might gain full beauty in the future. For abolishing all at once a tradition, practice, or law that is prevalent throughout the world and deeply established in human societies and institutions requires changing the essential nature of humanity. This is impossible and causes negative results. Consequently, the Shari'a did not legislate against slavery; rather, it saved slavery from savagery and amended it and put it in a form that would enable the emancipation of slaves and the complete abolition of slavery.

As for polygamy, the permission to have one to four wives has particular purposes and is not contrary to reason, wisdom, or essential human nature. However, the Shari'a did not increase the number of wives from one to four. Rather, it decreased them from many to four at the most. In addition, it laid such restrictions to having more than one wife that following these restrictions prevents whatever harm could possibly arise from polygamy. Even if it may cause some evil on certain occasions, it is the lesser of evils. The acceptance of the lesser of evils in the face of complete evil is relative justice. It is impossible for there to be pure good in every dimension or aspect of human life.

(From *Tulu'at* ["Flashes of Thoughts Rising in the Heart"])

In the face of rejecting the existence of a hadith

QUESTION: If one says, "I will not accept this *hadith*," how do you react?

ANSWER: Non-acceptance is sometimes confused with the acceptance of non-existence, and gives rise to many mistakes. Non-acceptance is reasonable if the necessary proof for the existence of something is lacking. But the acceptance of non-existence requires proof for non-existence. The former is a doubt, while the latter is denial. For example, a report attributed to the Prophet, upon him be peace and blessings, as a Prophetic *hadith* is either accepted or not accepted as such, or its being such is rejected.

The first requires proof. The second is not a judgment based on proof; it is ignorance or doubt. The third is refutation and denial, which requires proof; it is a negation, and negation cannot be proven easily. If the report in question is proven to be wrong in meaning or not attributable to the Prophet, its being a Prophetic *hadith* is rejected.

(From *Tulu'at* ["Flashes of Thoughts Rising in the Heart"])

Criticism, particularly in religious matters

QUESTION: How do you view criticism, particularly in religious matters?

ANSWER: What leads to criticism is either an attempt to calm anger and hatred in one's mind or to indulge compassion. Finding fault with a friend or enemy is an example of this.

A tendency toward acceptance or preference in a thing which is equally possible to be sound or corrupt comes from compassion, while an inclination toward rejection – if suspicion has no part – results from hatred.

> An eye of love and consent is blind to all faults,
> While an eye of anger and hatred sees only evil.

What motivates criticism should be love of truth and a desire to show the truth as being free from falsehood. The criticism made by our pious predecessors was of this kind.

(From *Tulu'at* ["Flashes of Thoughts Rising in the Heart"])

Index

176-178; functioning to veil the operation of the Divine Power, 4, 26; natural, 26-27, 101, 176; works of art refuting the creativity of, 26

Christianity, xvi, 6, 10, 31, 45, 47, 101-102, 114, 148

civilization; modern, 42, 46, 152; true, xx, 127-128, 169; vices of, 128; virtues of, 10, 125-126; Western, 10, 137

conscience, 4, 24, 29, 67, 77-78, 83, 92-94, 96-99, 111-112, 154, 157, 166, 173-174, 176 ; as the seat of belief, 78; point of reliance and the point of seeking help in, 173

Constitutionalism, xix, 143-145, 147, 159

consultation, xix, 134, 136-137, 143, 145; abandonment of, 136

creation; tree of, 88

criticism, 22, 75, 103-104, 109, 154, 163, 179; in religious matters, 179

Crusader, 102

curiosity, as the teacher of knowledge, 16, 71

D

Darulfünun, 77

Darü'l-Hikmeti'l-İslamiyye, 21

dervish lodge, 159-160

despair, xix, 16, 42, 71, 76, 92-93, 97, 108, 123, 130-131, 142-143, 166

despotism, xix, 36, 47, 141, 144-145

(Divine) Destiny, 39, 47, 93, 137

dignity, 9, 15, 40, 45, 68, 127-128, 146, 177; of Islam, 9, 40, 128

Dihyatu'l-Kalbi, 34

disagreements; among the scholars, 162

disposition; innate (God-given nature), 29

Diyarbakır, 156

E

ego, 8, 37-38, 67, 93, 102, 164

egotism, 37, 151-152

envy, 12, 16, 38, 55, 71

ether, 7, 33, 73

Europe, xvi, 9, 39, 47, 53, 84-86, 126, 136, 138-139, 147, 159

exaggeration, 50

extremes, of *jabr* (fatalism) and *i'tizal* (denying Destiny's role in our actions), 9

Ezra, 25

F

fame, 10, 50

(*Suratu'l-*)*Fatiha*, 23, 84, 88

(al-)*Fiqhu'l-Akbar*, 155

forgetfulness; as a bounty, 14, 67

freedom, xix, 8, 36, 42, 44, 47, 71, 102, 125, 127, 134, 137, 144-147, 159

French, 46

G

German, 46

ghazi, 91

gravity; providing the stability of the solar system, 27; sun's motion for, 27

greed, 52, 108-109

guides; spiritual, 155, 165

H

Hakikat Çekirdekleri, 21

heart; as the seat of belief, 78; point of help in, 94; point of support in, 36, 43, 94

Hell, xiv, 8, 13, 37-38, 58, 81, 93, 110, 130, 133, 152

heresy, 103-105

Index of God's Names and Attributes